stories of
MANHOOD

By the same author

The Leavin' School Game
Teaching About Youth Unemployment
The Contraception Game
The Secret of Happy Children
Manhood
Raising Boys

with Sharon Biddulph

More Secrets of Happy Children
The Making of Love
Love, Laughter and Parenting

stories of
MANHOOD

Journeys into the hidden hearts of men

Edited by

Steve Biddulph

FINCH PUBLISHING

SYDNEY

Stories of Manhood: Journeys into the hidden hearts of men

This edition first published in 2000 in Australia and New Zealand by Finch Publishing Pty Limited, ABN 49 057 285 248, P O Box 120, Lane Cove, NSW 1595, Australia.

03 02 01 00   8 7 6 5 4 3 2 1

National Library of Australia   Cataloguing-in-Publication entry

Biddulph, Steve.
Stories of manhood: journeys into the hidden hearts of men

ISBN 1 876451 10 6.

1. Men - Family relationships. 2. Masculinity. 3. Sex
role. I. Title.

305.32

Edited by Liz Goodman
Text designed and typeset in Garamond Book by *Di̇ʌ̃gn*
Cover design by *Di̇ʌ̃gn*
Cover photograph by David Moore
Linocut illustrations by Karen Johns
Printed by McPherson's Printing Group

Notes   The 'Notes' section at the back of this book contains useful additional information and references to quoted material in the text. Each reference is linked to the text by its relevant page number and an identifying line entry.

Photo credits   Simon McCulloch (p. 169), Rein van der Ruit (p. 177), Bill Brandt (p. 143)

Steve Biddulph's royalties from this edition are being directed entirely to The Fathers Project of Parents Advice Centres, a cross-community parents support organisation in Northern Ireland. This project encourages and strengthens fathers in raising their children safely and well.

Other Finch titles can be viewed at www.finch.com.au

Contents

Contents

I am the head of a statistically insignificant family. Our nucleus consists of a father and two boys. We three blokes (with no domestic role-model from the other side of the sex fence) represent a tiny, all-male proportion of the sole-parent family population.

It's such an unusual condition that you enter it only via catastrophe. Society and the courts consider mothers – rightly, in my view – to be so much the natural care givers that solo fathers rarely expect custody, and, when they are given it, they rarely remain single. So our family structure is the result of disaster – a death – although divorce also inflicted its own, more subtle, ongoing damage.

Alexander's mother, Susie, died in 1994 after a four-year battle with cancer. Hugo's mother had other problems; he came to join us a year later, when he was twelve, leaving my ex-wife to her new husband and their new children. But, at the start, there were just two of us – a middle-aged man and a five-year-old boy alone in a garden, on the day Susie slipped into a coma.

I said: 'You know how Mummy's been getting more and more tired because she's been so ill? We think she's gone into a very deep sleep now, and it's so deep we don't think she's going to wake up.

'In fact,' I said, taking a deep breath, 'we think she's going to die.'

'Is Mummy going to die?' he asked, more brightly than I'd expected. 'When?'

It was impossible for me to say, so he proposed some alternatives. 'Will she die by dinner time? Will she die by bedtime? By breakfast?'

A boys' world –
tears and all

Simon Carr

Simon Carr lost his first wife through divorce and his second to cancer. He ended up with one young son from each marriage and a steep learning curve as all three coped with the one thing traditional males find the hardest – grief. Added to that was another crippling handicap – Simon is English.

Totally unsentimental, this is a glorious story of ripped down defences, emotional honesty and muddling through.

What are the qualities of a good man today? Would he be a success in the conventional sense? How would we recognise him, what kind of job would he have? How do you 'do' manhood – what choices do you make? It's a struggle that every man alive – every teenage boy, every suburban father, every older man – is silently and privately fighting.

And this is the core of the problem – that men so often live their lives privately, isolated from each other by a tradition of silence, trapped by the culture and the demands of the economy like beasts of labour in separate pens. Even when men find answers, they are often not shared around. And when men suffer, they suffer alone. Suicide is the ultimate loneliness; following closely are alcoholism, divorce, poor health, crime and violence. The antidote to this poison is obvious. When we uncover our hearts, even just a little, we rejoin the human race.

The book that you hold in your hands is about men opening up as human beings. The stories are chosen for their exceptional and raw honesty, their protest, their bellowing of real pain and trumpeting of breakthrough in the business of being a man: anger at a botched vasectomy, pain at the loss of a loving partner, relief at surviving a peacekeeping mission, rage at sexual abuse, joy in the teamwork of man and woman, pleasure in the trust of a little child.

Stories are the currency of our humanness. They are like stones with which you can build the mansion of your own life. By reading about the lives of other men, we can broaden our definition of what masculinity means, love with more assurance, deepen our sense of humanity, and be part of the collective project to build a world worth living in.

Use these stories. Share them. Make something of your life.

Along with this idea that all the men of the past were domineering bullies, there arose its corollary – that sensitivity in men was some kind of new invention. Yet the men who fought at Gallipoli didn't lack tenderness. Nor did the POW's who cradled their dying friends in the mud and heat of the Burma Railway, risking Japanese bayonets and rifle butts to do so. They were capable of weeping, of breaking ranks in order to place a jungle flower on the grave of a mate. When the war finally ended, these men often found civilian life lonely and unreal, compared with the profound closeness of the prison camps.

Society evolves all the time. We should not blithely assume that life is getting better or we are becoming better people. History is littered with cultures that took a wrong turning into cataclysmic decline. Probably the truth is that we lurch in both good and bad directions. And with our global culture, these lurchings are huge and clumsy. It as if we were blindfolded, and crashing about in the china shop of our own humanity.

We have to take off the blindfolds, make choices, and examine closely what is sold to us as an economic inevitability. The nature of childhood is just one example of this. It's known that hunter–gatherer children – in the places where they still exist – are significantly more alert and intelligent than our own children. We know that children had larger and better vocabularies, even 100 years ago, than they have today: this is largely due to the fact that adults always seem to be in a hurry, and to the dumbing-down effect of television. We know that children had a healthier diet in the 1950s than they have today. While we hope we are producing a better kind of human being, we might equally well be doing worse – and we need to be alert to this.

When he was well into his seventies
He liked a few nights
At the local.
Andrew on his paper round
Used to head in to sell papers
And have a game of snooker
With Grandpa.
Needless to say, my children loved him.

Dad never swore in front of women.
One night one young hood
Was using the magic word with women present.
He didn't stop at Dads first warning
So Alas!
Left the bar with a broken jaw.

So this is the kind of man that is remembered with love and respect. Tough, uncomplaining, yet gentle with animals (well, most of the time!). Kind towards women and children, yet ferocious in protecting the ideal – of those times – of female sensitivities.

This image of a man – the honourable husband and father – was utterly denigrated in the 1970s ideology of postmodernism, and was recast as a patriarchal brute who dominated the family for his own gratification. (That there were abusive men, nobody doubts. But the simplification, the idea that most men lived by power and domination, or even wanted to, is an offence against the truth, and against the millions of men who strove throughout history to be honourable, protective, nurturing and fair. It is chilling to discover it in serious academic writings, or enshrined in government policy on domestic violence.)

held back from showing any physical affection, and left his daughter longing and yearning for it.

The fact that she treasures one fleeting memory of her father's touch, 60 years after the event, is unbearably sad. Yet Bill French's love got through all the same, and, years later, he comes to wonder if he did the right thing by being so constrained. He has the courage to share his misgivings with her, giving her the healing gift of understanding.

Val's father showed other qualities that were symbolic of the ideal man of the past. Here is another, more whimsical, poem.

I never doubted my father's strength.
Solid, tall farmer, strong as an ox.
We had a jersey bull called Glen.
Reared from a calf and quite a pet.
One day the pet turned nasty
And headed straight for Dad
Caught in the middle of a paddock
Dad picked up a huge stump
And as the bull got to him
He hit it over the head.
He brought the bull down on its knees
In a daze.
Dad walked out of the paddock.

His 21st birthday present was six draught horses
Nell, Darkie, E xer, Dollie, Bonnie and Blossom.
They worked ( ) the banks of the Murray
He was a gentle keeper
And they trusted him.

And so could a farmer. Bill French farmed the dry country of South Australia from the 1940s onwards. Here, his daughter Val Maslen, now in her sixties, describes him in a tender but wrenching poem.

One delicious memory I have
Imprinted physically and sensually
Which has withstood the years
Was as a five-year-old
Falling asleep on our straight-backed dining chairs.
My father six-foot-three and strong,
So very strong.
Picking me up and putting me to bed.
I can still feel his big arms around me
A loving sensation so wondrously warm
To a little girl
Starved of his touch.

Years later
When he was an old man
He told me he worried about being affectionate
With his three daughters.
He was concerned it may be improper or misconstrued
So he never touched us.
But ...
I always had that precious moment.

Living as we do in an era so sensitised to childhood sexual abuse, it's important to realise that other generations, too, were concerned, however awkwardly, to protect children. How poignant that, out of feelings of love and protectiveness, a father

Introduction

Steve Biddulph

We are often told that the role of a man is changing. Certainly on the face of it, this appears to be true. On the African savanna, or in Shakespeare's England, or on the battlefields of World War II, it might seem that different qualities were called for than those we would admire today.

Perhaps though, what makes a *good* man has not really changed. It seems to me that trustworthiness, a fierce capacity for love, unselfish action for the common good, and the ability to laugh in the face of hardship, were always what mattered most to a man's friends and family; that these qualities are in fact timeless, and acquiring them is as much the journey of a man today as it ever was.

Fifty years ago, being a 'real man' had a very clear and defined meaning. There were even well-understood types of men – people would describe someone as 'a man's man', or 'a bit of a ladies' man', or 'a real gentleman' (this latter term meaning someone who you could trust to be courteous and honourable). A swagman or a tramp could still be 'a real gentleman'.

Failing to find a time when Mummy might die by, and side-stepping, perhaps, the enormity of the event, he scampered away to tell his friend the next exciting instalment of his family saga.

The next morning, he came into the bedroom. His mother was lying there wearing a mysterious smile that had developed in the night. 'Did Mummy die last night?' he asked.

He was told. 'See!' he said. 'I told you! I told you Mummy would die last night!'

Everyone grieves differently. For weeks, Alexander compartmentalised his emotions, in the way you hear is particularly male. He would play happily much of the time, and talk about his mother in Heaven, calmly and affectionately. But he would also, on a daily basis, collapse into a kind of coma of his own - eyes open, registering nothing. Then, after an hour, he'd abruptly continue with his day.

Dealing with such emotions was new and not easy for someone with an untutored heart. I had never taken a proper interest in how these things work, and had been content to delegate much to Susie, who had real talent for how people felt. Taking stock of my limitations, it was obvious that I shouldn't attempt her way of doing things.

Being a real mother requires a whole set of neural wiring that men simply don't seem to have. So, rather than sit down with each other for a week and engage with the situation directly - as females might have done - Alexander and I loaded up the car with wetsuits, a small overnight bag, a pedal car belted into the passenger seat, a case of wine and two trays of beer, and went on a 500-mile drive around the country.

I am grateful to Alexander – as I was to become grateful to Hugo, too – for the emotional education he provided me. The tutorials started at once. One day, we were writing letters when I became short with Alexander (it's amazing, looking back through diaries of that time, how snappy I used to be – 'Do this! Say that! Watch it, you're pushing me!' – things I hardly ever say to him now).

He looked down at his paper and prepared his exit. My scramble to make amends came too late. Refusing to talk, he carefully crossed out every word he had written. Then, slowly, he got up and scuffed his way across the gravel to the courtyard gate. He opened it, and shut it behind him; I heard him gently, but lethally, shooting the bolt.

By some grace, I knew what to do. I ran across the yard and lumberingly climbed the eight-foot wall. He was standing there, very small, at the gate. I pointed at him and said loudly and unsympathetically: 'Oi! You! Open the door!'

'No!' he said, immediately struggling to conceal a smile.

'Oi!' I said, even more loudly. 'Open that door!'

With his hands at his chest, he bent forward in that way five-year-olds do. 'No!' he said. 'You're locked out!'

After I'd repeated my demand several times (at this age, repetition is the highest form of wit) the laughter started bubbling out of him like springwater.

There were other occasions when this counterintuitive burliness was the answer, and then there were times when sobbing and apologising was the best course of action.

For much of the following year, the two of us lived alone and I was absorbed by my work. Without my realising it, home became a bleak, boring and lonely place for a six-year-old. There was the television, and there were videos. But there was also my big back hunched over a screen hour after hour.

God knows, he gave me clues enough. He asked me to come and watch the video of Spielberg's *Hook* with him every night (it's about a neglectful father rediscovering his inner child). At bedtime, five nights out of six, he would ask for *Hannah and the Gorilla* – a story about a busy father and his daughter's secret friend. But he couldn't get his message across.

My solo-mother friends ran homes along Mrs Darling lines: warm and orderly, filled with the smells of casseroles and coffee and toast. At bedtime, the children brushed their teeth, got into their pyjamas and drank hot chocolate: in the morning, they got up early enough to wash their faces and have a big breakfast together. All in all, a very different set-up from our free-range and, at times, semi-feral regime.

One day, driving back from a visit to one of these more cheery households, Alexander said casually: 'Can I go and live at Belinda's?' He must have sensed this might be hurtful, because he went on: 'I could come back and visit you, so you wouldn't be lonely.'

I froze inside. Above everything else, I desperately wanted to say the thing that would make him want to stay with me. Instead, I said icily: 'You want to go and live there, do you? Go on then. You can go tonight.'

After which I slumped deep within myself and refused to say anything else. The expression on my face must have been grim

...I found myself sobbing, too, and loudly enough for him to hear up three flights of stairs...

indeed, because Alexander stopped trying to say anything else either.

When we got out of the car, he went upstairs to sob in his bedroom and I stayed downstairs in my study. Eventually, I found myself sobbing, too, and loudly enough for him to hear up three flights of stairs – the only way we apes had of communicating, each hooting to the other.

When I went up to ask him what he wanted to do, he wailed: 'Whatever you want me to do!' I was so grateful I couldn't believe my ears.

'What?' I said.

'*Whatever you want me to do!*' he wailed.

The reckless emotional free fall that I'd let myself go into was very damaging, and all the more so when Hugo came to join us. My feelings would gather like a meteorological depression, and it would only take some trivial remark on the part of Hugo to make me explode.

He would, for instance, come across some plan I was hatching for the weekend. 'I'd rather do that at Christmas,' he might say, 'to fit in with the school year.' Instantly, darkness would descend.

I had half-a-dozen such serious moods, each lasting a week, sometimes more. And the last was so bad that I sent Hugo back to live with his mother for a while.

His absence made me realise how essential he was to our emotional economy. He stayed away for ten days, until I finally got it straight in my head that he had to be treated a whole lot better, and be protected from these hurricanes.

How I controlled the moods I don't quite know. But I learnt to recognise their approach and avoid them – first, by agreeing with Hugo's objections (which were, more often than not, sensible enough), and second, by ruthlessly squashing any irritation I felt before it had a chance to develop into something larger.

These days, Hugo runs on a more even keel than any of us. When things get too much, he simply battens down the hatches.

Alexander, on the other hand, is more able to express his emotions. And while the pain is diminishing, it still occasionally makes itself known in some form or other.

Earlier this year, we were playing picture-in-the-clouds on the motorway when he announced that he thought we should get a convertible.

'You see that cloud that looks like a car that angels drive,' he said, matter-of-factly. 'If we had a convertible, or a car with a sunroof, Mummy could drop us messages down, couldn't she?'

In a way, of course, she is already doing exactly that – although the boys and I think we might just treat ourselves to the convertible anyway.

A small child's needs

Charles Fransen

I first met Charles in 1998 in Albury. Charles publishes a men's newsletter for the border region, 'Mankind News', where this mini-story first appeared.

Charles is a father first of all, and also a surveyor who negotiated with his company to work a four-day week for reduced pay. He combines work with parenthood as well as making a real contribution to his community.

It's misleading to talk about work–family balance, as if that's all there is. We have four essential aspects to our being – work, family, community and spirit. Neglect any one of these and you will fall over in the slightest breeze.

It is about 5 a.m. when I wake with a start. One minute fast asleep, the next wide awake. I hear my two-year-old daughter, Amy, coughing in her room next to ours. I vaguely recall my wife saying she had a tummy ache an hour before. The cough sounds a bit gurgly. The next thing I know, I am at her cot, helping her to sit up and finish throwing up. She's not upset because she is still mostly asleep. By the time she is properly awake, I am holding her, and she simply points to the mess in her cot and says quietly, 'Chuck up, chuck up'. I comfort her, clean her face, and take her to bed with us (mostly because I don't want to clean up her cot at 5 a.m.). She falls straight to sleep.

I wake later at about 7.30 to see Amy lying about a foot away from me and staring me in the face. She looks peaceful enough, but a bit worried. I smile and blow her a kiss. She smiles back and reaches out her hand to my face. I kiss it, and she reaches out the other to be kissed. Suddenly, not able to control herself any longer, she smiles, dives her face in to my shoulder and snuggles up to my side. I realise I will be late for work, but that seems so unimportant now as I lie and wait for her to fall asleep again. This she does almost immediately as she comes up for air in her sleep.

This is the sort of excuse that my boss doesn't listen to, so I don't bother explaining – it doesn't matter. What is important is the comfort and protection that children need from their fathers. What is rewarding is the love they give back. This is the sort of event that lets me get my perspective back. This is the sort of morning that reminds me of what is important in life.

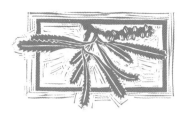

A small memorial

Peter Carey

Peter Carey is one of our most acclaimed writers of fiction, but he breaks the mould here in this autobiographical story. This is a spare and unforgiving confessional that will evoke strong memories in anyone who was young in the Sixties. What characterised this era was a great rush to explore new freedoms and possibilities – very often without the knowledge and safeguards (cultural or personal) to deal with them. Few of us came through this time unscarred.

The freeing-up process begun in the Sixties is now re-emerging as men are once again questioning their designated roles. There is a new willingness to look below the surface, to be more honest and less tame with our emotions. This story reminds us that the journey into grief is often the beginning of freedom, the beginning of wholeness.

Lately, when I think of my children, I have begun to remember not just the four-year-old who is rattling on my doorknob as I write, or the eight-year-old whom I will take to swimming lessons this afternoon, but those other children I have spent a long time trying to forget. These are the children from my first marriage, children now a long time dead.

In 1961, when I was eighteen years old, I sat in the waiting room of an illegal abortionist in Melbourne. Beside me sat an attractive, easy-going woman who would later be my wife but was at that moment my first girlfriend. Let us call her H.

There were many others waiting with us, but H and I felt alone and frightened. We knew we were at an abortionist's but it never occurred to us that all those other men and women (standing by the door, reading the *Sporting Globe*, the *Women's Weekly*) were also conspiring to terminate pregnancies. They looked married, respectable, not illegal at all. One woman, who had swollen legs and varicose veins, sat with a paper bag on her lap, knitting a green sweater. It was hard to associate any of these people with sex or the back seat of a car at the Star Drive-in Theatre, with any of the things that had brought us to this point where one of us might be injured, the pair of us arrested.

Years later, when we were both in our early fifties and were married to other people, H and I met for breakfast at the Melbourne Hilton, and she brought, as I had asked her to, photographs from our early days together. And it is because of these photographs, spread out before me now as I write, that it is so easy for me to recall H's open, fresh face, her handsome bones, her tanned skin, her curly, short hair. She wore a shirtdress that we incorrectly called a 'muu-muu', a light, striped summer dress that is somehow mixed up in my mind with the events that got us 'in trouble'. I wore a yellow terry towelling shirt and black and white checked trousers.

A year before, I had been at a boys' boarding school. Now, I was free, smoking cigarettes, having sex. I was an enthusiast, a compulsive talker, a would-be-cartoonist. I had an Ornette Coleman record called *Change of the Century*, which I played for H when I first met her – the track called 'Una Muy Bonita'. We may not have kissed that time, but still I'd like to think so, with Ornette Coleman playing in Melbourne in 1961.

In Melbourne in 1961, the bars closed at six o'clock at night. The White Australia Policy was still in force. You could be arrested for having an abortion or reading James Joyce's *Ulysses*.

H's brother had an MG-TD and a heavy Ronson cigarette lighter that bore a family resemblance to a Cadillac. He and his friends lay around the living room in the industrial suburb of Dandenong, lighting their farts with their Ronsons. They lay on their backs and drew their knees up to their chests. They stretched the fabric of their trousers tight across their bums. The farts burned with a sudden blue flame. H's brother had a pair of Cook's Daks; I can see them now with the blue flame shooting out of them.

I thought lighting the farts was infantile, but I knew the trousers were very cool. I bought a pair myself within a month of meeting him. (Thirty-four years later, you can still see the kitchen workers in New York City sitting on the pavement smoking, wearing trousers exactly like the ones I wore all through that spring, when I was busy falling in love, trying to be a poet, faking my experimental results for the force of gravity, busily on my way to flunking out of a science degree.) And I was still wearing them four months later, when I set out to procure an abortion, dropping the coins into the pay phone to call a doctor (whose name and address I must now alter). It was eight o'clock at night, and concrete trucks were rumbling past. I was about to ask this doctor to break the law, and I was both amazed at myself and terrified.

'Freddie,' I said when the doctor answered. 'It's Peter Carey.' He knew who I was, of course. He was a doctor in the beachside town where our family holidayed. His father had been my father's friend. He was Dr Colman - they both were, the father and the son, but they had been known usually as Dr Freddie and Young Dr Freddie. Now that the father was dead, the son had assumed his father's title: Dr Freddie. He was an educated man, young Freddie, and liked to say 'varsity' rather than 'university', which seemed to my ears most cosmopolitan. He was Catholic and lived in the same house as his receptionist, although I did not appreciate the nuances at the time.

'Hello, Peter,' he said when he took my call.

'Freddie,' I said, 'I think my girlfriend might be pregnant.'

'Okay,' he said. 'What makes you think that?'

'Her period is late.'

'How late?'

'Two months,' I said, 'and I was wondering: Is there anything you can do?'

There was a longish silence.

'I didn't know who else to talk to,' I said. 'I'm sorry, Freddie.'

'I think the best thing is, you should come and see me.'

'Tomorrow?'

'That's the trick.'

'Should I bring my girlfriend?'

'Not necessary, old bean.'

'Thanks, Freddie.'

'And, Peter, don't call me Freddie. You can call me Dr Colman.' When I hung up, I was no longer preoccupied by H's pregnancy, but by this last, mortifying rebuke. I felt fourteen fucking years old.

Next day, I drove south towards the town of Portsea, not to Portsea itself, but to a small town nearby. I sat in Dr Colman's waiting room, with the farmers and the retired men with white Panama hats and the young mothers from the Housing Commission developments, where the streets had names like Amethyst and Sapphire. My family had been coming here for so many summers, so may Easters, Christmases and weekends, that people I didn't know, total strangers, could tell me about the time when I was two years old and cut my foot on broken glass.

The contents of Dr Colman's office were as familiar to me as my own living room: the eccentric gas fire; the broken oar from a surf lifesaving boat; the ashtray made from an artillery shell; the photograph of old Dr Freddie standing on the beach in a black overall bathing suit; the cracked leather examination couch where I had the papilloma burned from my toe in extremely painful circumstances.

When I was finally admitted to the surgery, young Freddie sat behind his desk in his Harris-tweed sports jacket, smoking a Craven A cigarette. It was clear from the moment I walked in that he had decided what to do. He pulled a small pad of paper towards him and began writing on it.

'This is what we use as a test,' he said, tearing the sheet of paper off and sliding it across the desk to me. 'Just a little test.'

'Okay,' I said. 'Thanks. This is really nice of you.'

'Maybe she's not pregnant at all. So this is a test. Do you understand?' he asked me sternly, looking over the top of his glasses.

'I think she really is, you know. She's two months late.'

'It's just a way of making sure she's not pregnant,' he said.

'But if she is?' I insisted.

'It'll give her a period,' he said at last. He was a Catholic. Perhaps he did not like to think about what he was doing.

'Okay. Do I take it to the chemist's?'

'Yes, but not here. Take it to the city, that's a good bloke.' *

'Thank you,' I said. 'Thank you so much, Dr Colman. Is it okay if you don't tell my parents?'

He shook my hand. 'Just take it to the city, that's a good chap.'

I had a 1949 Armstrong Siddeley with leather upholstery, a sunshine roof, and a pre-selective gearbox of seemingly futuristic design. Six month later, this elegant old English car would fall apart and nearly kill me. It would slice off the top of my scalp and splash melodramatic blood all over my undergraduate poetry. But on this spring morning in 1961, it seemed to work just fine, and I drove it back to the city, my foot flat to the boards. I took the back road, with my arm out the window. The sky was a huge cobalt blue. I imagined our troubles were over.

What then happened in that Melbourne chemist's shop, I later made into an amusing scene in a novel, but at the time it was not amusing at all. The pharmacist looked at the piece of paper and said that it was not a prescription, because it did not have the doctor's name on it. He showed it to me. What he said was true.

My friendly family doctor had suffered an attack of cowardice too complicated for me to imagine even now. He had written the name of a drug on a plain sheet of paper but had neither signed it nor identified himself.

The pharmacist asked me if I knew what the drug was for. He asked this very loudly. I was an eighteen-year-old who looked so young that I often could not get served at Jimmy Watsons's Wine Bar. I stood there in the chemist's shop with my skinny arms straight by my sides, feeling the blood rising in my cheeks.

'Do you know what this does?'

I hesitated. 'Yes,' I said.

'I could call the police,' the pharmacist said. There were other people in the shop – grown-ups, respectable people, who turned to stare at me. I fled the shop, and I can still remember the feeling of panic, of wrong, of impending disaster as I rushed to hide myself deep inside the city crowds.

A few years later, abortion became a very public issue. There were police raids, judicial inquiries, pictures in the paper. The names and addresses of abortionists then became very public knowledge. But in 1961, the names and addresses were very much more difficult to obtain: a friend gave us a phone number scribbled on a torn scrap of paper.

H phoned the number from a public call box. A voice answered with a simple 'Yes?'. H nervously explained her 'situation', and we were told where to go and when, and to bring 50 pounds in cash. This was a huge amount of money in 1961. No-one we knew had 50 pounds.

Finally, however, we found a benefactor – one of my zoology professors. Professor T was a kindly man. He asked us to his home, and his wife cooked us dinner. Just the same, we were not surprised that he had taken legal counsel before making us the loan.

When we had those ten deep-blue five-pound notes, when we had found the waiting room, when H had submitted to examination, the news was still not good.

'She's three months' pregnant,' the strawberry-blonde receptionist said. She said this to me, not to H. 'We can't do anything without her parents' consent.'

'We've got the 50 pounds,' I said. 'We brought it with us.'

'Go away,' she said. 'Come back with her mother or father.'

This was 1961, but not yet the Sixties. If the Pill had arrived, we had not noticed it. It was before Haight-Ashbury, before Woodstock. It was, in effect, the Fifties, and teenagers were expected to keep their clothes on when in each other's company. To tell the woman, whom I will call Mrs Z, that her daughter and I had had sex was just unthinkable. To say that she was pregnant was to imagine a disgrace too shattering even to contemplate.

But of course we did. We did it as we had done the other things, as we had borrowed the 50 pounds, rung the doorbell at the abortionist's. We did it on a quiet suburban afternoon in Dandenong, in a comfortable, untidy house that I had come to think of as my second home.

We sat in the kitchen and drank tea. Then one us said it. Which one? I don't know. One of us opened our mouth and made the words come out. H's mother was sometimes given to picturesque upset, but she took our news calmly – far more calmly than anyone could have anticipated.

If we had been a littler older, a little less frightened, we would not have been so surprised: in the suburban world we lived in, this was a woman famous for her eccentricities. As a teenager, she had attempted to flee an isolated bush town carrying nothing but an unloaded revolver. She had mailed her wedding invitations with the wrong date on them, on purpose. She did not like housework – dishwashing, dusting – and she had been known to leave unfolded sheets lying in the laundry for months on end. She did not make the bed. She kept a five-foot-high stack of newspapers in the kitchen, waiting until she would have time to read them. This was before feminism, and there was no-one to tell her that this behaviour was okay. She did not care.

This was not, I now see, a woman who was going to persuade her eldest daughter to begin life as a mother at the age of twenty. Thus she quickly became our co-conspirator, and when it was time to go back to that single-storey Victorian terrace house in G Road, she came with us. While the abortionist's receptionist counted the 50 pounds, Mrs Z stood by our side. When H went in for her operation, Mrs Z sat with me in the park.

And there, on a park bench, in the sunshine, my future mother-in-law and I talked. Doubtless I was being insensitive, but when she said, 'This doesn't happen from doing it just one time,' I decided not to hear the question she was really asking me. I remember being relieved that we were so companionable and easy with each other.

While we sat on a park bench, H lost her baby. I met her afterwards in the waiting room. She was strangely unchanged and yet also changed absolutely. She was pale and shaky, lost in her own pain. We drove back along the Princess Highway, down through the industrial suburbs with incongruous names like Noble Park, to Dandenong, where poor H went to bed with a hot-water bottle. I don't remember what lie we told her father. He was a good and decent man. I still stand, guilty and embarrassed, in his imaginary presence.

I don't think H and I ever talked about that baby, and yet I don't think, given the choice all over again, that we would have done any of it differently. She must have grieved for the child, but she never said so, and I was young and callow and it would not have occurred to me that she might.

Our hearts were not broken, and we went on to our new young marriage, and our new young lives. H was 23, and I was 21. We travelled the world – Asia, the Middle East, Europe, London.

We came back to Australia, to three-quarters of an acre and a little house. We planted hundreds of trees – eucalyptus, acacias, melaleuca. We were ready to begin our family. I had a job in an advertising agency and wrote short stories at night. H was working at the Red Cross. We were now 27 and 29. That had been so long ago.

H quickly became pregnant. I remember her slowly swelling belly, the nights by the log fire, the feeling of domesticity, the certainty of how my life, or life, would continue.

This was 1970, and the world was changing. We were active in the Vietnam Moratorium Committee and knew that our phone was tapped. We were socialists. Our bookshelves were stuffed with Franz Fanon and Regis Debray, but also Becket, Faulkner and Ursula Le Guin. We played 'Blonde on Blonde' so loudly that it rattled the windows and yet our own expectations of life were anchored in the Fifties. Neither of us expected that H would have a career. She had been a gifted philosophy student but had dropped out of university to become a photographer's assistant. And, while she was a talented photographer, she was never particular ambitious. She could take things or leave them. She could lie in the sun. She liked to pursue abstract philosophical puzzles. In her forties, long after we split up, she began to study cartography, and when I think of her doing it, I imagine her pursuing her studies with fascination and wonder rather than with ambition. H had a placidity and an intelligence that I, with all my nervous energy and extravagant dreams, found enviably sexy.

She did not feel ambivalent about abandoning a career to have children. It was our plan, and, as her belly grew, our plan became more and more real. There were no birth classes, no pre-birth education of any type, but there was our baby: we lay in bed and felt it kick.

H says it was summer, but in my memory it was autumn. The frosts had not arrived, but it was still cold enough to light the fire. It was around midnight, the ashes in the fire were grey, and the house had lost its heat, when H shook me awake.

I can still see that bedroom: its unadorned convict brick walls, its long jute curtain. I turned on the light – a single naked bulb that stuck out from its black Bakelite fitting on the wall.

'My waters broke,' H said.

'The waters can't have broken. You're only five months. That doesn't happen until the baby's being born.'

'Well, everything's wet.'

It was. In harsh, unsentimental light, I could see that the sheets were sodden, but I would not believe that what had happened could happen. 'Maybe you peed.'

'It's not pee. My waters broke.'

We phoned the doctor, and he said he would meet us at the hospital, some twenty minutes away. The thing is this: we did not know what was happening. We had not the least damn idea. We locked the house and bumped down the steep clay track and drove out along gravel roads into the suburban night.

I could direct you to the hospital now – Lower Plenty Road, Heidelberg Road – but I forget the suburb's name. It was a small, suburban redbrick hospital near a railway line, but I don't know what it was called.

And there, in a single hospital room, my wife went into labour. She had not been in labour before. Was this labour induced? I have no idea. At the time, I knew less. Did we know we were losing our child? Yes, we did. No, we didn't. We knew because we were told, but we did not believe it because of the pain, its endless pulsing contractions, because of the birth taking place. I held H's hand but did not know how else to help her. And when, finally, I was sent away, I left gratefully and stayed in a neon-lit corridor that still keeps pushing its way into my fiction.

But then the baby was born, dead. Did I see her? No, and yet I sometimes imagine that I did. It is mixed up with the next time – and there was a next time, although that night we did not know there would be one.

Let me tell the next time now, too. Let it stand for both times, because in truth the two have become the same in my memory.

We had accepted that there was 'something wrong' with the first baby, that it was 'right' to lose it, but we did not know that more babies would die before this story would be over – that it would be years before H and I would meet in the Melbourne

Hilton and show each other, along with photographs of our youthful selves, baby photographs – babies from our new marriages.

When we were still married, we did not know that the 50 pounds the strawberry-blonde woman counted so carefully had also procured an 'incompetent cervix', which was why the next pregnancy repeated itself like a sequence from *Last Year at Marienbad*. It unwound its long, sickening strand of story in the same bedroom, with the same convict brick walls, the same bare light bulb that still had no shade to soften what it showed.

Like all nightmares, the repetition was not exact. This time there were twins, and when the labour was over, they were alive. The nurse emerged from a door and asked me if I wanted to see them. I was again in that damned corridor.

I was afraid.

I walked through a door, and there they were – a boy and a girl, with perfect little hands and faces. They were tiny, and delicate, but there was nothing wrong with them. They had familiar family features which I would later recognise in my sons. I stood and watched our beautiful babies in the oxygen tent and could not believe that they would die.

> I stood and watched our beautiful babies in the oxygen tent and could not believe they would die.

To the nurse, I said, 'Will they be alright?'

'Oh, no,' she said. 'Oh, no.'

How long did they live, my babies? I swear, I do not know. How could I have been so ignorant? I think only that I fled the pain, that we fled the pain, the knowledge, chose not to remember.

I could not bear to know what it was we had lost. I sat with H in her hospital room.

'Did you see them?'

'Yes.'

We wept together; we wept for our loss. Obviously I was not heartless. And yet, when I tell you the next part of the story, I fear that I will appear so.

It is eleven o'clock in the morning, and I am sitting in a funeral home with Mrs Z. We sit on one side of a desk, the funeral director on the other. He is a man of 50, with a grey sweater underneath his suit. I am a writer of unappetising short stories, with a pasty face and long hair that needs a wash.

He sits, this man, and asks me how I want the twins buried.

I am not religious, and I cannot bear the religious smell of the funeral home, the flowers, the unctuous voices, the false comfort. Dead is dead. To put a name on plaques, to say prayers – all this is lies, bullshit in the face of the nothingness of death. And in believing this, I am at one with my wife who, even as we meet with the funeral parlour man, is taking the first of the pills that will dry up the painful milk that has come to feed the dead babies we are discussing.

Slowly we go through the options. We agree on cremation. We agree that the ashes will be put in a wall. I do not ask where the wall is or what it looks like, but I imagine it to be made of damp red bricks with doors like a set of mailboxes. It is an enduring image – one I will be able to see clearly long after I have forgotten the funeral director's face.

'And what names?'

'No names,' I say.

'Are you sure?' my mother-in-law asks.

'I don't believe in God,' I say.

It is not the point, of course. She knows it is not the point, but she sees the fierceness and fragility of my grief.

'Later,' she says gently. 'Later – don't you think you might be sorry?'

Surely she is thinking of her daughter, of what she would feel herself.

'Are you sure you won't be sorry?'

It's later now. Looking back on Australia in 1961, I feel I grew up in a dark and ignorant time: a racist immigration policy, great works of English literature banned, abortions performed furtively, illegally, not always well. When I look back on how our story went, H's and mine, I don't really see that it could have gone any differently.

I wish only that we had honoured those children with a plaque, a name. I will always wish that, forever.

The horse
I backed

Michael Leunig

Michael Leunig's work has evolved over the years – from political cartooning, to whimsy, to trenchant commentary on the depths beneath our daily lives. Australians have given his work their highest honour – to be placed on a million refrigerator doors. He may be the closest thing we have to a spiritual leader. As new forms of oppression spring up, he unerringly exposes them: economic rationalism, crêche-reared babies, pomposity and viciousness masked as self-esteem. Yet (with the possible exception of jet skiers!) there is no aggression in his cartoons, only compassion with honesty.

This cartoon is at the heart of the men's liberation message. The world's machine says to you, 'Work till you drop; spend till you are satisfied' (though you will never be satisfied). Jump the fence. Make your own path through life. You won't be sorry.

The only horse I ever backed turned and ran the other way.

At the very start it turned and jumped a fence and was gone from sight!

A week later I saw it, high in the mountains, still going strong; it leapt a huge chasm and disappeared into the mist.

About a year later I saw it struggling through heavy seas, far from land but looking good; looking good.

years passed and then I saw it galloping through a terrible fire. I saw it crossing a great desert. I saw it chased by mad dogs. I saw it in a green pasture; it was looking good — looking good.

The horse I backed took a different course.

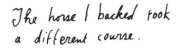

It's a snip

Ian Hargreaves

Simple and painless – that's how vasectomy is usually portrayed. It's a contraceptive option chosen by tens of thousands of men every year. But some of these men have discovered that the risks of the operation are greater than they had been lead to believe.

No medical procedure is without its risks, and it's important that every man considering vasectomy be properly informed of them.

In this article, a leading British journalist shares his personal, and painful, experience.

The leaflet from the Marie Stopes Institute was reassurance itself. The operation was 'safe, simple and effective ... the worldwide recommended family planning method for men who want a permanent solution to their contraceptive needs'. A diagram illustrated the procedure: an incision of 'less than one centimetre in the scrotum' through which the tubes which carry sperm to the ejaculatory liquid would be cut and cauterised. 'Does it hurt?' the pamphlet asked. Foolish thought. There would be a local anaesthetic of the type dentists deliver every day, although, like dentists, 'we cannot guarantee you will feel no discomfort'. Afterwards, there might be 'a dull ache which can be relieved by taking paracetamol'. And the risks? 'Vasectomy is very safe and long-term effects are extremely rare.' Although there was (and is) talk of a link between vasectomy and prostate cancer, 'there is no conclusive evidence'. It would take a real sissy to say 'No' to this.

The operation, the pamphlet continued, should not be considered reversible (although in the hands of the right surgeon, it mostly is), but it would not adversely affect my sex life or my ability, after just four weeks, to take part in violent games. 'Many couples find greater sexual freedom once the risk of unwanted pregnancy has been removed', the writers of the pamphlet seemed to whisper.

I felt quite relaxed when I arrived at the clinic, which turned out to be a Swansea general practice. The jolly nurse who greeted me was surely, someone I had seen in *Carry On Nursing*; any moment now, she'd bathe me in a shower of double entendres. Instead, she sat me down and asked me to confirm how many children I had fathered. Guilty as charged. 'You've obviously made your mind up about this,' she said. Counselling session over.

Having been instructed not to arrive in loose-fitting boxer shorts, but in briefs, I removed those and lay on the couch. Now the doctor joined the nurse and explained that there would be a modestly uncomfortable local anaesthetic, followed by the operation. I should inform him if the situation approached agony.

The nurse talked about her religious convictions and her social life. The doctor joined in, telling me about his fondness for sea diving and explaining the difficulties he was having in resurfacing his driveway. 'No molten bitumen today, though, eh?' I quipped. The smell of burning had meanwhile become strong and persistent, and the physical sensation that of an electrician rooting through a hole in the ceiling for recalcitrant wires. Somehow, things didn't seem to be going to plan. The nurse's accounts of her evangelical convictions became more florid, but less distracting. After 40 minutes, I was told to re-hoist the briefs and to 'take it a little easy for a couple of days' and everything would be fine.

The next morning, I was black and blue across my entire groin area, bleeding spasmodically and walking like an extra from a John Wayne film. It was a fortnight before I felt anything like normal, and I waited for a subdued but nagging pain to subside.

I also waited for certification that I was now infertile. After the specified twelve weeks, I started to fill the plastic sample jars with ejaculatory fluid for testing at the lab. On Christmas Eve, I had a letter: the sperm were still at large. They would need another series of samples. I was upset.

What was really bothering me, I think, was the sense that an operation which many men plainly find unproblematic had become such a trouble for me. Why was this? Five months after the operation, I still had pain every day. I thought back to a Friday afternoon in Swansea and reflected upon the laying of bitumen and about what they used to call 'Friday afternoon cars' in the dog days of British Leyland.

> Five months after the operation, I still had pain every day.

I sent off more samples. By March, another letter – still the sperm were defiant. I telephoned MSI to say that I was concerned that the operation had not been well-conducted, that I was not feeling well and that I would like to see a specialist in London to discuss the matter. An appointment was made.

I arrived at Marie Stopes House itself, in West London, where *The Guardian*'s 'Woman of the Millennium' had set up her family planning clinic in 1925. At first, I didn't realise that I had been booked in at the start of an afternoon devoted to the breaching of more male vas deferens, but because the doctor turned up 90 minutes late, there was plenty of time for conversation in the small, nervously packed waiting room.

There were three couples and me.

'You first then, mate,' says a man in a leather jacket. 'Don't use up all the blades.'

'It don't hurt,' says a woman on the opposite set of chairs, looking as if she were fresh from snapping telegraph poles across her knee.

'You know anyone's actually done this, mate?' inquires leather jacket.

'Well, actually, yes,' I say. 'I've had it done myself.'

'So, why you here then?'

'Because it didn't work.'

The silence that followed was charged.

'Whaddya mean, didn't work?'

'Well, I had the operation last summer, and I've still got positive samples. But I've come here today because I've also been in a bit of pain.'

'Pain, whaddya mean? They say it's no problem.'

'Look here,' says the telegraph pole-snapper. 'I don't think you should be coming in here upsetting all these people,' glancing at her petrified husband.

'He asked me why I was here,' I say. 'I told him.'

Silence resumed.

Eventually, the consultant urologist turned up. He looked at my 'notes' – the form I had originally filled in, with boxes marked to record the results of my prodigious supply of samples. I asked him if he knew anything about the doctor who had done the operation. 'Can't read his name,' he said.

I described the intermittent pain in my right testis. 'There is a risk of chronic pain after vasectomy,' said the consultant. 'Some people experience pain for their whole lives, but the numbers are very small – 0.1 percent.'

'Why does your literature not make this clear?'

'Because the risk is so small, we are not required to state it.'

'What about the fertility issue: what is your conclusion?'

'It appears that the operation has not been successful. You still have one more sample to complete, but it does not look very hopeful.'

'What are my options?'

'You can have another operation, under general anaesthetic.'

'What effect will that have on the pain?'

'It's unlikely to make it better, but it's difficult to say.'

As I grumbled back down Whitfield Street, I was not feeling too warm towards the author of *Married Love and Wise Parenthood*. I would do something I'd never done in my life: I would seek a second opinion.

A general practitioner friend inquired on the consultant urology circuit and referred me to Mr Chinegwundoh at the London Independent Hospital. He told me, and put in writing, that he tells his vasectomy patients that the incidence of chronic testicular pain is 4 percent. He confirmed that I would probably need a second operation to become infertile.

The only thing I knew for certain was that I was not going to trust a surgeon to undo the problems caused by surgery. Perhaps I should

> He told me ... that he tells his vasectomy patients that the incidence of chronic testicular pain is 4 percent.

sue, but where would that get me, other than an unknowable distance down the path of vengeance? I resolved to live with it. To moan silently, and brood. The brooding moved in two directions. One was the peevish mood which thought ill of an organisation which campaigns so hard for its birth control mission that it puts a dubious sales gloss on medical evidence. On the other hand, I couldn't complain too much. Compared with the dangers women face from sex and reproduction, vasectomy is hardly a big deal. Childbirth is not without risk. Even in thriving, Blairite Britain, female sterilisations, of which there are about 50,000 a year, involve a risk of fatality, chiefly through the effect of anaesthetic.

Although there is a man on the Internet setting up Men Against Vasectomy (having coughed up $185,000 in fees to deal with the aftermath of his own operation), there is not really any good evidence for claims that vasectomy raises the risk of genital cancer or other ailments.

What there is, however, is a clear risk of chronic pain. In my case, this is still intermittent and irritating rather than debilitating. If I had known this risk, I would probably still have had the operation. But why is it so difficult for medical people to understand that most patients prefer to be fully informed?

Men are to blame, too, preferring the maximum in jokes and the minimum in useful conversation about these matters. If you doubt this, look at the men's health websites – vasectomy is simply not an issue. And how often is it discussed even in the ubiquitous health and lifestyle features of the newspapers?

Yet, since my own snip, I've found that almost every man I know has either had or been obliged to consider having a vasectomy. Men, though, prefer to talk about football or the Third Way or the decline of the BBC. One friend told me the other day that, having had a vasectomy some years ago, he is now undergoing expensive fertility treatment to have his blocked sperm released into a test tube so that his current partner can try to have a baby. When the subject is raised with men who haven't yet succumbed to the pressure to have a vasectomy, they usually wince, as when seeing a batsman catch a fast inswinger just inside the thigh. Then they look smug.

But even if we become more enlightened, there are no grounds for thinking that the vasectomy curve leads irresistibly upwards. For one thing, there are big national variations – perhaps vasectomy is even a crude measure of the private power of women in a society. In France, it is almost unknown. In the US, it is now the second most common form of contraception (after condoms), with 500,000 operations a year. Adjusted for population, that is twice as many as Britain's 50,000, which, curiously, has been steady since the early 1980s. About 11 percent of British men, mostly in their thirties and forties, have had a snip, compared with 12 percent of women (aged 16 to 49) who have had the more complex and traumatic sterilisation operation. Almost everywhere in recent years, consumption of the Pill has tumbled (a British survey of clinic-users found it dropping from 70 percent in 1975 to 44 percent in 1997), while use of the condom has gone up, thanks to anxieties about sexually transmitted disease. We can and do change our birth control techniques.

My complaint against MSI and other such organisations is that they cannot be trusted to guide our choices because they are propagandists as well as service providers. Earlier this year, MSI published the results of a survey said to confirm its own view that vasectomy is a low-risk, painless procedure. Only a quarter of the men asked agreed that the procedure was 'very good/effective/professional'. Had the respondents experienced any continuing problems? Almost 9 percent said they had.

By the way, I had another letter from MSI the other day. It was headed, 'Congratulations!' and continued: 'I am pleased to inform you that the last two semen samples you sent showed no sperm present. You may now stop using other forms of contraception, as your vasectomy has been successful'.

No, brother

Leo Schofield

Leo Schofield is a prominent and delightful Australian who seems to oversee almost everything cultural in this country. Many know him best as a food writer, arts critic and director of major arts festivals.

In recent decades an horrific pattern of sexual and physical abuse of children has emerged in schools and institutions, church and secular, across the globe. Organisations charged with the utmost care of children have harboured the worst mistreatment. We have barely begun to bring to light the extent of this, and responses have been far from adequate in taking responsibility, bringing perpetrators to account, or making just reparation.

Unlike many of the children affected, Leo Schofield was fortunate in having a father who discovered his abuse and who stepped in to end it. In September 1996, at the height of the controversy, he wrote about his experiences in a courageous and moving disclosure in *The Sydney Morning Herald*.

We called him Itchy. No-one knew who had given him this nickname or when, but everyone, even the ten- and eleven-year-olds under his care in sixth class, knew why. Even now, 50 years after I walked through the gate of the Christian Brothers school in Sydney's inner west where I received my secondary education, I marvel that his superiors never twigged to his goings-on or, if they did, why they never cautioned him or attempted to curb his behaviour. His fellow teachers must surely have known of his propensity for touching up little boys. And some parents must have had wind of his exotic behaviour.

Yet it was never spoken of, except by us kids who swapped stories of violent beatings, smutty talk, wandering fingers, the chilling sensation of his powerful left arm encircling one's juvenile waist, drawing one towards him, pressing one's slim, boy's body against his own fuller form while whispering obscenities into one's ear.

Itchy was not a pleasant-looking man. Of average height, rotund, bald and with a pink pate, he resembled a malevolent Friar Tuck. His milky skin had a sheen on it like that of a freshly sucked sugar pig. His pink-rimmed eyes protruded slightly, giving him the alarmed look of a

His milky skin had a sheen on it like that of a freshly sucked sugar pig

laboratory rat. But despite his ill-favoured appearance, he projected a dazzling self-confidence. His walk was a swagger. His voice a booming announcement of self-importance.

His background was hazy. He had come from New Zealand. One rumour had it that he had played for the All Blacks, another that he had studied medicine (he routinely wrote out prescriptions, usually for himself), yet another that he had a steel plate in his head from some injury or other. His rages were often put down to the pain experienced when the plate expanded and contracted inside his cranium.

Another part of the Itchy myth was that back in the Shaky Isles he had been cruiserweight amateur boxing champ. He may well have been, but had there existed a Lonsdale Belt for flogging, he would certainly have won it.

'You boys get it easy,' he told us often. 'When I was teaching in New Zealand, the temperature overnight used to drop below zero. I used to soak a length of rope in brine and then hang it out on the clothesline, and in the morning, when it was good and stiff, I'd use it on those lads who'd been naughty the day before.'

In the absence of his preferred icy, brine-soaked rope, Itchy used a short leather strap, standard Christian Brothers issue, not dissimilar in outward appearance to that used by his colleagues. There was, however, a significant difference. Itchy had his custom-made by the local bootmaker who had a shop just near the local railway station. Between the two pieces of thick boot leather, the cobbler inserted, under Itchy's watchful direction, two or three used hacksaw blades. The other brothers' straps were flexible. When they descended on the hand, they exhibited a modicum of pliability. But Itchy's strap was rigid, heavy and hard, and few things in life seemed to afford him as much pleasure as using it.

Encountering some innocent child in a corridor or play-ground, he'd abruptly ask: 'Have you had the strap today, boy?'

'No, Brother.'

'Hold out your hand, then.' *thwack ... thwack ... thwack*

No reason was ever offered for these unprovoked and violent assaults. One might have minded them less if they had been deserved. But violence was an accepted part of the Christian Brothers culture, at least at the school I attended.

It is probably too much to expect fit, healthy males in the prime of life to suppress all temptations of the flesh and still remain stable. Yet among the men who taught me in the late 1940s were many selfless, honourable, patient souls who seemed to be able to manage to do just that and who, perhaps naively, actually saw their God-dictated sacrifice of life, marriage and career as rewarding. But among them were also monsters who believed that knowledge was best transmitted from teacher to pupil by means of a length of leather.

Now, in the late 1940s, the relationship between the inflicting of pain and suppressed sexual impulse was imperfectly understood, certainly not discussed publicly. Few recognised Itchy for what he was: a slightly unhinged thug and a pedophile who should have been removed from any contact with young boys. Instead, he had free and unimpeded access to his victims and a fresh crop every year.

He favoured nice-looking boys but slow-learning kids. Those who mucked up in class or even failed to answer a question satisfactorily were daily called up front to his desk and offered an option. 'Six on the hands or three on the bot?' he would ask his victim with a smirk. No-one wanted cuts on the hands.

Three on the left, three on the right from that steely strap and one's hands were so swollen that one couldn't write for an hour, so most opted for three strokes on the backside. At least one could soothe the resulting pain by rubbing one's arse up and down on the curved, varnished seats attached to our desks, and still continue to work, although it was sometimes difficult to see the pages of our school books through tears.

Having made the inevitable choice, the victim, trembling, would follow Itchy into the adjacent empty science lab. There he was instructed to drop his short trousers, bend over facing the bench, steady himself against the top with his hands and present his pink backside for punishment. As he did so, Itchy produced his obscene strap, which he usually kept, like Arlecchino's phallus, up the sleeve of his shiny black soutane.

There followed a kind of foreplay as he thrust this surrogate penis between one's legs, diddling it around tiny, undescended testes, gently drawing the strap upwards between the cheeks of one's backside. Then, suddenly and silently, he'd swing it up excitedly into mid-air and bring it down with extraordinary force in an almighty horizontal cut across juvenile buttocks. Again. And again. Each time, the foreplay became more protracted and more varied and the subsequent blow more forceful, often so strong that it drove one's pelvis hard up against the side of the bench or sent us flying sideways to the floor.

The pain was excruciating and nine times out of ten the recipient would begin to cry at the first stroke. But we never liked the rest of the class to think of us as sissies. Wiping away tears on a shirt sleeve, we pulled up our pants, tucked in the shirt tail and contritely trailed Itchy back into the classroom.

None of his victims that we knew of ever told his parents about Itchy's shenanigans, his gratuitous dirty talk, his twiddling with our little dicks.

Retrospectively, I can only ascribe the reluctance to do so to fear of reprisals. Many parents would not have believed the stories anyway. They saw the Brothers as living saints, holy men who had given up their lives and the prospect of parenthood to the thankless task of educating children and, more importantly, to maintaining the Faith. The conspiracy of silence was breathtakingly maintained until the recent airing of similar unpleasant practices by others more damaged than myself. But some parents, mine included, found out about Itchy's tricks by other means.

As I was getting into the bath one evening, my father spotted three angry purple-black weals across my backside. He asked me what had happened. I told him. He blew his top, called my mother to witness the bruises, uttered a stream of fearsome curses.

Dad and Mum discussed the matter. We had no telephone so Dad decided to go up to school with me the next morning to confront my assailant. Fearing reprisals, I begged him not to do so, but he was determined to have it out with Itchy.

The next morning, grim father and white-faced son boarded the train together, alighted together, walked together to the Brothers' residence, where he rang the door bell loudly. A housekeeper in a floral cross-over pinny opened the door. Dad announced himself, asked to see the Principal.

We were ushered into the parlour, a fusty, umber room where parents were interviewed about problem children, news of expulsions were broken to them, discussions held on their sons' prospects. How long did we wait there? Probably no more than four or five minutes and yet every detail of that room became etched in my memory for life.

Into this drab brownish world burst the Principal.

'Can I help you, Mr Schofield?' he asked politely.

'You certainly can. Take a look at this,' replied Dad, signalling to me to drop my pants, an action which, through repeated response to Itchy's orders, I was able to accomplish in jig time.

I turned around, faced a statue of Sainte Therese of Lisieux in her regulation brown habit, black veil, cross embedded in a Tosca-like bouquet of pink plaster roses and with a face like Paulette Goddard, undid my belt and dropped my duds.

The Principal appeared shocked and asked the skinny woman in the pinny who had been hovering around to find out what was going on, to fetch Itchy.

I was still in the corner, facing Sainte Therese, my pants like hobbles around my legs, when he walked in. I spun round to confront my tormentor. Arrogant, dressed in brotherly black but with a pair of comfy checked carpet slippers on his fat feet, he came through the door clutching a large white damask napkin with which he dabbed residual bits of boiled egg from the corners of his mouth.

Something about his demeanour triggered the fuse of Dad's quick Irish temper. If anyone was going to lay into his son, it would be him, not this smug, shiny-pated, black-habited prick. Dad sprang at the startled man, grabbed him by his collar and lifted him off the ground so that the toes of his checked slippers barely skimmed the pseudo-parquet.

What little colour there was drained from Itchy's face like the liquid in a spirit level stood suddenly on its end.

'Listen, you bastard,' cried Dad through clenched teeth. 'If you touch my kid again, I'll ram your f-----g teeth down your throat, even if you are wearing a f-----g dog collar.'

'Mr Schofield, Mr Schofield,' cried the Principal, attempting to come between Dad and Itchy. 'I can understand how you must feel, but there is really no call for this kind of behaviour.'

Dad was staring Itchy full in the face. Slowly Dad lowered the offending brother to the floor. Itchy retreated like a rat scuttling into a crack, back to his embarrassment and his half-finished egg. Assured that no such beating would ever take place again, Dad prepared to leave. I quickly pulled up my pants, hoicked up my school socks and was ushered out with my father.

For the rest of my year in his class, Itchy never touched me again. In fact, I can't even recall that, after his confrontation with my father, he ever looked me full in the face. But

'Listen, you bastard ... If you touch my kid again, I'll ram your f-----g teeth down your throat ...'

he remained at the school and there were others he subsequently molested.

I'm not sure how I feel about the scandal surrounding the Christian Brothers today. Exposure was inevitable and it is surprising that it has taken so many so long to speak up, but speak up they have in large numbers and loudly. And the Order has been besmirched, probably irretrievably.

Not all of the Christian Brothers interfered with their youthful charges. And while Itchy remains, after five decades, a recurrent nightmare for me, one of his colleagues, Caesar, has been a lifelong inspiration, a brilliant man and a brilliant and selfless teacher who rose to be a distinguished leader and, finally, Secretary of his Order in Rome.

Some little time before he died, Caesar was in Sydney and I arranged to have afternoon tea with him at the café in Centennial Park. We had not met or spoken for more than 40 years, but he remained an unseen force in my life and I had written affectionately about him in a piece for the *Herald*. A reader forwarded a copy of that piece to him in Rome and, as a consequence, a reunion was arranged. He was old and frail and his formerly jet black hair was white, but his mind was as sharp as it had ever been.

I was overcome with emotion at meeting again this man who had been so supportive, so generous, so influential in my youth.

I had planned to broach the subject of Itchy with him and tell him how traumatised I and other kids had been, but I simply couldn't bring myself to do so. I wanted to ask him if he knew what was going on, if he simply prayed that the problem would go away, if he felt that it would reflect so badly on the Church and the Order, if he and his colleagues admitted to knowing about such things, that they kept mum. But these matters remained unaired. I sensed he knew I might ask an awkward question or two, or blurt out an unpleasant truth, and something in his manner suggested such behaviour might be unwelcome.

How fortunate that Caesar died before the scandal in which the Christian Brothers are now mired erupted.

Things we wouldn't know without TV

John J Pungente SJ

What's wrong, little boy? You don't have a father? No men in
your life? Don't worry – television and movies will teach you
all you need to know about being a man!

1. The importance of guns, and how nothing can hurt you

- One person shooting at twenty has a better chance of killing them than twenty people firing at one.
- Stripping to the waist makes a man invulnerable to bullets.
- If you need to reload your gun, you will always have more ammunition – even if you weren't carrying any.
- If you do run out of bullets, just throw the gun away. Guns are like disposable razors – you can always buy a new one.
- You can always find a chainsaw (or steel fighting rod, stout cudgel, fire hose, or lightning bolt, depending on the universe you're in) when you need one.
- If being chased through town, you can usually take cover in a passing St Patrick's Day parade – any time of the year.
- A person being pursued will always stop to throw something at the pursuer, even though it takes longer to throw the obstacle than it does for the person chasing to jump over it.
- If you're heavily outnumbered in a martial arts fight, your enemies will patiently dance around in a threatening manner until you've knocked out each of their predecessors.
- A gang of highly trained terrorists (or police, soldiers or starship officers) will always separate and search for an intruder (terrorist, criminal, nasty alien creature) on their own so they can be killed off one by one.
- The ventilation system of any building, submarine, spaceship, etc. is the perfect hiding place. Your pursuers will never look for you there, and you can move to any other part of the building, submarine, spaceship etc. without difficulty.

- Cars being pursued will always crash into at least half the other vehicles, lampposts, garbage bins, etc., in their vicinity and keep on going.
- Cars that crash will almost always burst into flames.
- A man who shows no pain while taking the most ferocious beating will wince when a woman tries to clean his wounds.

2. Understanding people

- Even when they're alone, foreigners (or alien species) prefer to use English to speak to each other.
- Anybody wearing a bow tie will be British.
- Any high-class stripper with a heart of gold can operate most heavy machinery.
- A cough is usually the sign of a terminal illness.
- When a person is knocked unconscious by a blow to the head, they will never suffer concussion or brain damage. However, even the slightest blow to the head is enough to cause amnesia.
- No-one involved in a car chase, hijacking, explosion, volcanic eruption or alien invasion will ever go into shock.
- An electric fence, powerful enough to kill a dinosaur, will cause no lasting damage to an eight-year-old child.
- Any person waking from a nightmare will sit bolt upright and pant.
- Medieval peasants had perfect teeth.
- Interbreeding is genetically possible with any creature from elsewhere in the universe.

3. Cops and robbers – a rough guide

- Police investigations require at least one visit to a strip club.
- Detectives can only solve cases once they've been suspended from duty. So, the star detective will always be suspended or given just 48 hours to finish the job.
- Police departments give their officers personality tests to ensure they are assigned partners of opposite temperament.
- Honest, hard-working police officers are traditionally gunned down three days before retirement.

4. Wars and other disasters

- Should you need to pass yourself off as a German officer, you don't need to speak the language. An accent will do.
- If your town is threatened by an imminent natural disaster or killer creatures, the mayor's first concern will be the tourist trade or his/her upcoming art exhibit.
- You're very likely to survive any battle in any war unless you show someone a picture of your sweetheart back home.

5. The importance of pets you can depend on

- All single women have cats.
- Dogs always know who's bad and will bark at them.
- If you think there's an intruder in your house, your cat will choose that precise moment to leap out at you from inside a cupboard.

What price compassion?

Mohamed H Khadra

Mohamed Khadra is a leading Australian surgeon. Three years ago, the roles in his life were suddenly reversed when he was diagnosed with a fatal variety of throat cancer. His experiences – the sudden admission to a public hospital, the degradation of that experience and the insight that he gained from it – were published in the *Medical Journal of Australia* in 1998, attracting wide discussion. Mohamed subtitles his article 'a personal view of care in our public hospitals'.

There is much discussion lately about why men do not access health services. There is no mystery. Men don't like humiliation. We don't like to be vulnerable, in a place where that vulnerability is not supported. No institution (except perhaps our prisons) is as ripe for fundamental change as is our public hospital system.

I have cancer. There are cells dividing in my body which may hasten that day, perhaps a day in the not-too-distant future, when I will shuffle off this mortal coil. But I do not dwell on death. I have seen traumatic sudden deaths, and I have seen the slow and tormented deaths of the old and sometimes the young. I have come to accept death as a release. I have pondered about the journey. I have wondered about God. I have made my peace.

What concerns me now is life.

The time is 4.30 a.m. It has been a long night; my pain has not abated since 2 a.m., despite medication. I am in a hospital, lying on a rubberised mattress, with matching pillows, on a bed which screams in agony each time I move, as if it too has had enough. The walls of the room are bare, but not featureless – their surface a collage of paint and no-paint. As patients before me have left this room, they have taken with them a small souvenir – a patch of paint stuck to the tape that attached their memories to these walls. I have sat for hours imagining the pictures, paintings and sayings hung on these awful walls. I do not need to stretch my imagination to do this. I recall the artefacts my patients bring to hospital. Pictures of families, as if to say, 'I know I am only a patient, but I am human too. See, here is my family to prove it.' The point is never proved. 'Patients' are no longer free, individual spirits. We are an imposition which opposes the basic focus of modern hospital life – shifts which end on time, completed paperwork and balanced budgets.

I am a bit cold. The aircell blankets are never long enough to cover all of me. Maybe there are cogent reasons for choosing them, but I yearn for my doona, and for my wife. Our life together is interrupted each evening by a clanging bell. She leaves and I remain. I wonder then if I will see her again. I wonder if this is the night when I will arrest and need to be resuscitated. It would be ironic to arrest on a bed where ten years ago I had resuscitated others.

I finally get to sleep. The door suddenly opens and there is noise and a blinding shaft of light. It is the cleaner. She walks in, removes the contents of my garbage bin, replaces the lining and leaves. I get up and close the door. Why can't she knock, and close the door when she goes? I say nothing. My head is now throbbing. She screams to her colleague down the corridor. I can hear the clanging of the drug trolley approaching and the sound of sphygmomanometers being pumped across the corridor. I get the feeling that I should be awake now. Rise and shine, cornflakes time.

The door opens again and the light shines in. 'Just going to do your blood pressure.' The thermometer goes in under my tongue. The nurse places his fingers on my radial artery. It is strangely comforting to feel the touch of another human. I look into his eyes. He is pleasant, good-looking, about twenty. A skull-and-crossbones earring hangs from his left earlobe, his haircut is a bit weird. I struggle not to be judgmental. He is doing his job efficiently. The sphygmomanometer is pumping up and he has his stethoscope pressed against the artery. The pressure comes down and I feel the first few spurts of blood ejaculate down my occluded arm. How gratifying that my heart is still functioning. I look into his eyes again and he averts his gaze.

'Do you need anything?' he asks.

(Yes, there is much I need.)

'No, I'm fine, thanks.'

(I need you to sit with me for a while. I need to tell you what a lousy night I have had. I need you to put your hand on my shoulder and cry with me. I want you to fear my fear, feel my pain, doubt the future. I want you to wonder with me what my funeral will be like. I want you to tell me that my wife will be all right without me. I want you to tell me that lots of children grow up without a father and that mine will cope. I need your compassion. I need more. I need your very soul bared to me so I can bare mine to you ...)

I turn in bed, discomforted by these thoughts.

I know there will be a period of quiet soon. The round will be done, the cleaners will retire for morning tea and the nursing handover will begin. It is not a good thing to need anything at this moment. All of us patients know that our duty is not to interrupt this process, at any cost. Woe to the patient who dares to use the buzzer now. Hold on to your bladders, grit your teeth, live a moment longer.

I get up for my shower. The bathroom is shared and there is liquid on the toilet seat. I clean it off and sit down, hoping it was only water. It takes a while to start these days. I look around. The shower curtain is mouldy and there is a hand-held shower in a big deep bath. I get in. For the first time since I've been in hospital I get a total body hug. The shower curtain is wrapped around me. I am nauseated. All I can think of is the thousands of patients before me who have been hugged by this very curtain – the open sores ... the colostomies ... the drain fluids ... the urine bags. I can't stand any more. I squat in the shower. The hot water running off my back mixes with the scalding of tears running down my face. My body shakes in uncontrollable mourning and shame.

I was a medical student, an intern, a resident, a registrar, and now I am a consultant ... and I never knew what this was like. I have done early-morning ward rounds. I have woken patients from their sleep to examine them. I have switched on the overhead lights at two in the morning. I have sat down in the middle of the nurses' station and had a laugh in the middle of the night, especially during those 60-hour shifts we used to do when I was an intern. And recently I have sat with patients and sentenced them to death. I have patted the backs of their hands and left their rooms.

It is suddenly so clear to me. Compassion – a basic ingredient – is missing.

> I squat in the shower. The hot water running off my back mixes with the scalding of tears running down my face.

Compassion in a hospital is as essential as the delivery of nursing care, of medication, of meals. A hospital is a meaningless edifice if even one patient we are caring for has pain which is not eased, has a sleepless night, is given an unwholesome meal, is in unaesthetic surroundings or is treated without basic human dignity. And compassion is not the doctor's monopoly.

Everyone who steps into a hospital to work needs a daily reminder of its raison d'être.

There are so many administrative layers in the hospital now that it seems, from where I lie in my hospital bed, that the institution has been built to serve the administrators' needs and not mine! I can see the nurses spending hours filling administration-required forms at the end of my bed and at their station. I see the nursing unit manager spending most of the day going to meetings and writing in gigantic ledgers which, in turn, others study.

How do junior doctors and nurses find a role-model of compassion and care? Who is it that they observe during their own personal and professional development? Are we rewarding those around them who show compassion? Not so. The reward for good workers in a hospital is to elevate them to ranks within the administrative hierarchy, where, instead of allowing them more freedom to care for patients directly, the reverse occurs. They can free themselves of the burden of direct human contact. This has profound ramifications – the message is that direct human care and compassion are activities from which the healthcare worker must strive to escape. You are penalised in the modern hospital environment if you spend extra time with a patient and as a consequence your paperwork is not done. This alone is a powerful message that compassion is not a priority.

What is compassion if it is not time and care? Woe betide the charge sister if her overtime budget is exceeded. The cleaners on a tight schedule may be penalised if, by knocking at each door, they work more slowly. A nurse who senses, while taking a pulse, that the patient needs time to speak about his or her illness, knows that if the time is taken to listen, there will be penalties for being late for report. The intern on morning rounds has only a short time to see that all is well on the wards before theatres. No power on earth should deter one from being on time for theatres.

Perhaps modern healthcare cannot afford compassion? Perhaps it does not fit into the corporate model of patients as clients, nurses as managers, doctors as visitors and administrators as the pinnacle?

Or perhaps these are just the idealistic ramblings of a narcotised mind.

Either way, the bell has tolled. My wife is leaving with all the other visitors. She has brought in a picture painted by my son. I tape it to the wall in front of my bed and lie down. If I leave, I will take some of the paint with me as a reminder of my visit.

Once again, I am left to face the night alone.

Spare the rod

J J Bell

I came across this touching story, written in a kind of Gaelic accent, in a book called *Growing Up in Scotland*, a collection of historic accounts of childhood from that brooding land.

Even in the 1880s when this account was written, the rights and wrongs of hitting children were very much an issue. And the challenges of parental cooperation were just as daunting then as they are today.

It was evening in the cottage. The meal was over. Everything was tidied up. On the right of the hearth sat Mr Brown, his uneasy countenance concealed by a weekly paper; on the left sat Mrs Brown, cold and stern, knitting steadily. On a stool, set apart from his relatives [his uncle and aunt], squatted John. *The Pilgrim's Progress* was on his knees, and his eyes were glued to it, but he had not turned a page for half an hour.

There had been a long silence, broken only by the wail of the wind in the chimney, when Mrs Brown spoke.

'Peter, the time has come.'

Her husband started. Behind the paper he muttered: 'I canna dae it.'

'It's yer duty.'

'Weel, I'll see aboot it in the mornin'.'

'It's got to be done the nicht, an' the suner the better.'

'Oh, woman,' said Peter, in a lowered voice, 'let it pass this time.'

'Spare the rod an' spile the child!' she retorted.

'Fudge!' Peter let fall the paper, possibly in astonishment at his own temerity.

'What?' exclaimed Mrs Brown, as one who refuses to believe her ears.

'There was plenty o' the rod afore he cam' to us,' said Peter, 'an' what guid has it done?'

'Peter,' said his wife, 'if ye dinna dae yer duty, ye'll be sorry.'

Peter knew he would be sorry either way, but habit reasserted itself and obedience followed. He cleared his throat.

'John,' he said ponderously, 'I was vexed to hear ye had been a'tamperin' wi' yer aunt's eggs. What for did ye dae it?'

John, looking wretched, answered nothing.

'Tamperin'!' exclaimed Mrs Brown. '*Stole* is the word for't! An' eggs that few an' valuable!'

'Maybe he didna ken he was stealin',' said Peter. 'Did ye, John?'

'I – I thocht the hens wud lay plenty mair, Uncle Peter.'

'Ye had nae business to think what the hens wud dae,' his aunt said bitterly. 'Peter, he's confessed to stealin' hauf a dizzen in the last twa weeks, but he wudna confess what he did wi' them. Ask him!'

'John, what did ye dae wi' the eggs?'

No answer.

'There ye see!' cried Mrs Brown at last. 'If he had confessed, I micht hae overlooked it. Dae yer duty, Peter, as ye promise me ye wud. It's for his ain guid.' She paused. 'I'll gang oot to the hen-hoose till ye get it ower.' She nodded in the direction of a cane, commonly used on carpets, that stood against the wall beside his chair, where she had placed it earlier. Then, taking up her shawl and a candle, she left the kitchen.

'The Lord help me!' sighed Peter, and added under his breath: 'I wish I had Solomon here.' Without looking at the boy, he said: 'John, will ye tell me what ye did wi' the eggs?'

'I canna.'

'Weel, I'm damn – I mean, I'm exceedin'ly sorry, but I'll hae to punish ye – gie ye a lickin', in fac'. Prepare yersel'!'

'Hoo am I to prepare masel'?' quavered John.

With a sudden inspiration, the man pointed with the cane to the red cloth on the table. 'Tak' it an' wrap it roun' yer legs.'

A new form of torture, perhaps, but John obeyed.

Mr Brown advanced and took his victim carefully by the coat collar.

'Noo mind,' he said, 'I've got to try for to hurt ye. Ma duty, ye ken,' he added, rather apologetically. 'Are ye ready?' He flourished the cane and brought it down gingerly on the tablecloth. 'Did that hurt ye?'

'Ay - na, it didna, Uncle Peter.'

'Honest lad!' A slightly harder stroke. 'Did that?'

'Na.'

After several cuts, the tormentor paused, looking helpless.

'Uncle Peter,' said John, 'ye'd best lick me proper, or she'll no' be pleased wi' ye.'

'Tits! Ye'll break ma heart. There!' (*whack*) 'Was that no sair?'

'A wee bittie.'

(*whack*) 'An' that?'

John winced.

'It wud be better if ye cried oot,' said Mr. Brown, and struck once more. 'Yell!'

John gave a squeak. Then suddenly, 'Oh, Uncle Peter, ye're awfu' kind,' he said, and fell to sobbing bitterly.

With a bad word, Peter flung the cane across the kitchen. 'God forgi'e us a',' he muttered, and unwrapping the cloth, replaced it on the table.

'John,' he said, and patted his nephew's shoulder, 'dinna greet. This'll be a secret atween us. An' I'll tak' yer word if ye promise never to gang near the hens again, excep' by yer aunt's orders. I suppose ye sooked the eggs - a natural proceedin' for a hungry juvenile in cauld weather. An' ye'll tell yer aunt ye're sorry, an' try to mak' it up to her – eh?' Unable to speak, the boy nodded emphatically.

'Guid lad! Tell her the morn, an' gang to yer bed noo. Oh, wait a meenute! Here's anither secret. Tell naebody.'

John felt something put into his hand and himself guided from the kitchen. In the passage, Peter took up a small safety lamp and carried it into the box of a room where the boy slept.

'Guid nicht, John, an' forget yer troubles,' he said and closed the door.

After a while, John opened his hand expecting to find a ha'penny – and lo and behold – a shilling! It was long – for a little boy, at any rate – before he slept, but when slumber arrived, it found him perfectly happy, for everything had come right.

When Mrs Brown returned to the kitchen, her husband, from behind the trembling weekly paper, managed to say:

'His sufferin's was terrible, Elizabeth. I hope ye didna hear him.'

She sat down as though very tired and moistened her lips.

'I had ma fingers in ma ears,' she said.

Gender relations, Dilbert-style

Scott Adams

Every airport bookshop in the world has a rack of books about business success: how to manage like a Mohican, sell like a Samurai, and have one-minute orgasms to manage your time better. (I made that last one up. Sorry.)

The most intelligent, perceptive, and practical of this whole genre are undoubtedly the comic Dilbert books, which outsell (and at the same time, spoof) all the competition.

Jesters are vital for restoring the sanity of a culture. They have a way of showing us that our glib assumptions about life might not be altogether true – such as, for instance, the assumption that men control the world.

In the future, women will run the world in all democratic countries. I base this prediction on two facts that cannot be disputed:

1. Women already control the world.
2. Who's going to stop them?

Men live in a fantasy world. I know this because I am one, and I actually receive my mail there. We men like to think we're in charge because most of the top jobs in business and government are held by men, but I have a shocking statistical insight for you men - *those are OTHER men*. The total percentage of men in those top spots is roughly 0.0000001 percent of the male population. I'm not one of them. I just draw cartoons and write these stupid books. Chances are, if you're a man reading this, you're not running the world either.

I have about as much in common with the CEO of a Fortune 500 company as I have with my cat. It's not logical to say that I, as a man, run the world based on the fact that total strangers with similar chromosomes have excellent jobs. Yet that is exactly what many people believe.

When the Joint Chiefs of Staff are deciding whether to go to war, they do not call my house and say, 'We're calling all the men who run the world to ask for their input'. Believe it or not, they make those decisions without consulting me ...

Someone might argue that men have access to the top jobs whereas women do not. There's some truth to that, but the mathematical fact is, 99.9999999 percent of all men can't get those top jobs, either. There aren't enough of those jobs to go around. The rest of us men live in a world that is ruled by women, as I will explain for those of you who hadn't noticed.

What evidence do I have that women rule the world? Take a look at the world and ask yourself how it would be different if men were *really* in charge. Look at the things that men want most, then check to see if the world is organised to *provide* those things or to *limit* them. Logically, if men made the rules, the world would be organised to provide them with the things they want most.

Men want sex. If men ruled the world, they could get sex anywhere, anytime. Restaurants would give you sex instead of breath mints on the way out. Gas stations would give sex with every fill-up. Banks would give sex to anyone who opened a checking account.

But it doesn't work that way, at least not at my bank. (Having your own 'personal banker' isn't all it's cracked up to be.)

Instead, for the most part, sex is provided by women if they feel like it, which they usually don't. If a heterosexual guy wants sex, he has to hold doors, buy flowers, act polite, lift heavy objects, kill spiders, pretend to be interested in boring things, and generally act like a complete wuss. Can anyone think men designed *that* system?

If men were smart enough to figure out what's going on, they might be tempted to use their superior size and strength to dominate women. But women are too clever to let that happen. Thousands of years ago, women figured out they could disguise their preferences as 'religion' and control gullible men that way. In one part of the world, I imagine the conversation went like this:

HUSBAND: 'I'll be back in an hour. I'm going to covet my neighbour's wife.'

WIFE:	'You can't do that!'
HUSBAND:	'Why not?'
WIFE (thinking fast):	'Um … God said so. He's an omnipotent being. If you don't obey him, you'll burn in hell.'
HUSBAND:	'Whoa, that was a close one. Thanks for warning me … How about if I kill her husband first?'
WIFE:	'Ooh, bad news on that, too.'

Religion is only one of the ways women control men. It runs much deeper than that.

≈≈≈

Courtship

Under our current system of courtship, men do most of the date-asking and women get to squish men's fragile egos like Fudgsicles on a Los Angeles freeway. I'm reasonably certain that men did not invent this system.

If it were up to men, all women would be equipped with special hormonal monitors to tell men such vital information as when it's a cry-free time of the month and when arousal is highest. Then we'd know when it's a good time for courting and when it's a better idea to run some errands. This would be a huge time-saver for everyone, but obviously nobody consulted men about how courtship should work.

Money

On average, men get paid more money than women. Most people think that is unfair, but let's look at it another way. Given a chance, most people would rather spend money than earn money. And who is doing all the spending?

If you don't believe that women spend most of the money, just walk into any Sears store and see what they're selling. If you're a male, you see maybe two things you might want – a second cordless drill (so you have a spare in the car) and a trickle charger, because you like how they look in the garage. That's all you want in the whole store. But *someone* is buying all that other stuff in there or Sears wouldn't be in business. Someone is buying those fuzzy toilet seat covers. Someone is buying decorative covers for tissue boxes. Someone is buying place mats.

Who could it be?

Kids don't have money. Pets aren't allowed in Sears. By the process of elimination, we can conclude that women must be buying all that other stuff. Women are spending most of the money.

If you were from another planet, such as Switzerland, and you only knew these two facts –

1. Men earn most of the money, and
2. Women spend most of the money,

what would you assume about who is holding whom by the whatchamacallits and swinging the person who owns the whatchamacallits around in the air while yelling, '*I am woman, hear me roar!*'?

It's a rhetorical question.

Fashion

If men controlled fashion, they'd convince women to wear uncomfortable pointy-heeled shoes that made legs look attractive. They'd promote bras that lifted the breasts upward for no apparent reason. The standard business attire for women would be skirts that display lots of leg. Men, on the other hand, would be able to get away with wearing a dull grey suit or jeans every single day.

Actually, I guess that's the way it is. Obviously, men control fashion. But that's the only thing men control.

Old recipe, new recipe

Michael Leunig

At what point does self-esteem cross over into arrogance? Does a person have to put others down in order to put themselves up?

Another of life's secrets laid out in a six-frame cartoon. If men and women can't be humble, then they can never be close.

So, you're one of those single women, 30-40 years old, who can't find a good man and think that men are too stupid to appreciate what a ravishingly brilliant creature you are; who think that men are too dull and cowardly to engage your vivacious, intelligent spirit, your proud confidence, your sheer excellence and the awesome richness of your experience and achievement. Don't despair. The answer could be quite simple. For instance, has it ever occurred to you that you might be too pompous? Or just too greedy and brattish; or too sanctimonious and hypocritical; just too up yourself and full of bullshit? Has that occurred to you? After all, it's quite natural to be like that — utterly human!

Or have you considered that you might not presently have the capacity to recognise a good man even if you saw one and that a good man mightn't want to go near you with a forty foot pole because you are such a screeching, nasty, scolding tyrant; a pain in the neck, a crashing bore and a sly, ruthless megalomaniac? Just imagine that! After all, it's perfectly normal to be like that; perfectly human; and fairly forgivable too; eventually.

However, if you want a mate, you've got to know how to cook — how to cook up a good relationship. It's no good dreaming one up in The lounge room of Excellence; you must prepare for ordinary, hard slog: you must roll up your sleeves and cook one up in THE KITCHEN OF GIVE AND TAKE.

FIRST YOU MUST CLIMB INTO THE BATTERED OLD SAUCEPAN OF LOVE WHERE YOU WILL MARINATE IN THE SAUCE OF SEX.

NOW YOU ARE TOSSED IN THE PAN OF CHAOS AND SEARED BY THE FLAME OF TRUTH

ONTO THE PLATE OF ACCEPTANCE AND GARNISHED WITH THE HERBS OF HUMILITY.

THEN YOU SHALL BE COVERED WITH THE WINE OF FAITH, THE OIL OF COMPASSION AND THE SALT OF SIN AND SUFFERING.

YOU ARE CARVED BY THE KNIFE OF COMPROMISE AND SERVED WITH THE SPOON OF DUTY;

AT THIS POINT YOU MAY WELL SAY GRACE.

Leunig

My goofy brother

Michael Pollard

The YWCA's Big Sister/Big Brother program matches up children who are in need with adult, same-sex mentors. It is a carefully supervised program of friendship and activity that endeavours to give these youngsters enhanced self-esteem, wider horizons and the opportunity for a better life as a result.

Michael Pollard has been a 'little brother' for five years, and in this piece, he speaks very perceptively about the effect the experience has had on his life. The giving is two-way, otherwise the program would make no sense at all. In reading this young man's words, you too will derive benefit – a sense of vitality and clarity about life comes through very strongly.

Details about the program are included in 'Notes' at the back of this book.

My mum and dad split up when I was very young, and I didn't see my dad for a long time. The only man in my life was my grandfather, who I was very close to. My grandfather died when I was about twelve, and I started getting into a bit of trouble. Maybe I was taking out my anger on other people.

I was living with all women, I had no male role-models. My mother is a smart woman, and when she heard about the Big Brother program, she thought it might be just what I needed. It wasn't until only a month before I met my Big Brother Joe that I found out that she had put me on the list to be matched with a Big Brother. I was quite nervous about meeting someone totally different, but I didn't say 'no'.

I remember the day Joe first came around to the house. He was waiting out on the front lawn for Shauna, who was the organiser of the program at that time. One of my little cousins came in and said, 'There's a strange man on the lawn'. We went out and saw this goofy-looking man there. He introduced himself, and I quickly decided he was a really nice guy.

It's hard to say what I've got out of having a Big Brother, because I don't know how it would have been if I hadn't been with Joe. But I know definitely - if it wasn't for him, I'd have been in a lot more trouble.

The first time I went to court, for assault, Joe got me a lawyer, and he asked me to promise him that I wouldn't get into trouble again. I could see how much he cared, because I knew that he didn't have to do this if he didn't want to. But he made the effort to get me out of trouble because he cares, and I thought that if he's making this effort, I have to make the effort to keep myself out of trouble, too.

When I made a promise to Joe, I felt I had to keep it.

Around Riverwood where I live, it's very easy for boys to get involved in gangs. There's nothing new about that – gangs have been around for a long time, but the gangs are getting bigger and into more serious crime. When I was a kid, we might see a pair of shoes outside a house and someone would run up and steal them. Now I've got a friend who's going to court for stabbing someone in a home invasion. He's a really small guy, who wouldn't have the courage to do something like that on his own, but when the gang gets together, they gee each other up. 'Let's go rob a bank,' and if someone says 'no', they don't want to, they get called a pussy, and eventually they do it. They suck each other into it.

Gangs are about being territorial. If you're a teenager around here, and you're not from Riverwood, you're a threat. If one of the Riverwood guys spoke to you and you gave a smart-arse answer, you'd probably be bashed. Someone from another area hanging around another gang's territory is like someone coming into your home uninvited.

Some suburbs have a bigger gang problem than others. You don't see them on the North Shore, because around there you don't have to do crime to get money to entertain yourself. A lot of people around here don't have jobs, and they do crime to make money.

It's also because people around here have a lot of time on their hands and don't know what to do, so they hang around on the streets and make trouble.

There is a good side about gangs, and that is loyalty. I know there is always someone watching my back, and someone from a gang will always protect another member no matter how dangerous it is for them.

I finished Year Ten at school, but because my grades weren't good, I went to TAFE to do a Certificate of General Education. My plan was to join the army, but I injured my back and so I won't be able to do that. My auntie is starting a trucking business, and I'll be getting a share of that. I'll be working as an offsider until I get my licence.

In the meantime, I've been building a granny flat in the backyard with the help of two friends. We mixed the cement by hand day after day for a long time! I'm living in the granny flat now with my girlfriend.

Having a Big Brother has meant I can do a lot of things I would have missed out on otherwise. There are things you can't ask your mum to do, like go and watch a football game. But with Joe, I go to the footy, go rock-climbing, four-wheel driving, golf – stuff you can't do with females. Some things, like golf, my friends would not be into, so I would never have tried them if it weren't for Joe. I was surprised, but I enjoyed golf! Another time, Joe and his brothers helped me learn to do back-flips and now I can do them really well, especially on the trampoline. At the Men's Leadership Gathering in Tasmania this year, I helped teach a lot of older guys how to do them, too. It was mad!

As well as doing things together, there were lots of times when Joe gave me advice that helped me get through hard times. He told me that I should treat others the way I would like them to treat me. I hadn't realised that before – it was always just me and my friends against everyone else who I treated like shit. At first, I just said, 'Yeah, whatever', and ignored what Joe was telling me, but after a while I matured and it started to sink in. Nowadays, I actually listen to what people say, because I've learned that some things can be helpful.

There was one incident which I particularly remember. When I was fifteen, a friend and I robbed a guy our age on the street. I ended up in court. Joe was really shocked; he couldn't believe I would do this after promising him to keep out of trouble. He asked me why the hell I did such a stupid thing, and I said, 'I wanted to teach him a lesson!'. He was really angry and said, 'And what do you think he learnt? You're the one with serious criminal charges, police and courts turning your life upside down, and he's at home taking things easy. Yeah! He's really learnt his lesson, hasn't he?'

I think Joe has learnt some things, too, from being with me. I've never lied to Joe because he's never lied to me. I don't think he realised how hard life can be for teenagers until he understood where I was coming from. He learnt that if you're a teenager, you don't actually have to be doing anything wrong for the police to pick on you. I've been searched by the police for just sitting on the corner doing nothing. Once I was playing basketball with some friends and because the clothes I was wearing matched the description of someone else who had just done a robbery, the police slammed my head into a wall, handcuffed me and searched me. When I told Joe what had happened, he was furious, and he managed to get me a written apology from the police.

I was lucky to have a Big Brother. I have spent every Sunday for the last five years with Joe. I have met his family, who have all accepted me, too. We will be friends forever.

My life is in pretty good shape. I've got my own place, a girlfriend. I'll soon be earning money. In a few years' time, I see myself having a good job, a nice car, being married and living in a nice apartment.

I'm lucky to have a plan for my life. A lot of my friends have had their future planned out for them – they are already in jail and they are staying there. Maybe if they'd had Big Brothers too, things might be different for them now.

Happiness

Quan Yeomans/ Regurgitator

Frank Pittman, renowned family therapist, has this to say about teenage music: 'Try to listen to their music. You can't be expected to live with it – it loosens the wallpaper ... and defrosts the refrigerator. But the lyrics help you to better understand how scary it is to be an adolescent.'

Ninety-nine percent of teenage music today is created by men in suits packaging up alienation and rebellion like a soft drink to sell in shopping malls. It's no wonder that kids feel disoriented, when even rebelling is complying. But, all the same, music lives and creativity shines through.

The first thing to know about teenagers is that when they say, through their behaviour, words, or attitude, 'I don't care' – it means they do. These lyrics from Quan Yeomans of the Australian band Regurgitator show lots of care. 'I got a speck of truth caught in my eye. It stings like hell and it's making me cry.'

I love pointless effluent, it seems to love me.
Sticking to my teeth like polythene glue,
making everything seem so sweet.
Big wide world of bitterness, baby,
poisoning up this tongue.
Give this life its sweet respite,
let's rip that packet of fun.

Rotting my brain once again.
It's always the same and it never ends.

Love me, lovely cathode ray,
mother me in your glow.
I'll do anything you say,
if you tell me I'll never be alone.
Touch me shiny magazine,
touch me way down there.
I can't help imagining,
that you really care.

Rotting my brain once again.
It's always the same and it never ends.

Drug me, fuck me, dull the pain, I don't ever want to know.
Knock me down and I'll get up again,
you know that I'll do what I'm told.
I got a speck of truth caught in my eye.
It stings like hell and it's making me cry,
But getting up would only leave me wondering why
everything's turning grey …

Rotting my brain once again.
It's always the same and it never ends.

The sporting life

Bill Bryson

Bill Bryson's hugely popular books about travel include *Notes from a Small Island*, *A Walk in the Woods*, and *Down Under*. His humour can sometimes mask a gentle outrage against the stupidities of the modern world, and this outrage is very close to the surface in this piece about the direction sport is taking.

Sport used to be a real boon for families, because it helped so much with our goals for raising our kids. It was all about character, fun, challenge, fitness and belonging.

Not any more – unless we quickly come to our senses.

We have a friend, a single mum, whose six-year-old son recently signed up to play ice hockey, a sport taken very seriously here. At the first team meeting, one of the other parents announced that he had devised a formula for determining how much each child would play. Essentially, the best seven players would play 80 percent of each game, and the remaining, more hopeless kids would divide up whatever time was left – so long, of course, as victory was not in doubt.

'I think that's the most fair way of doing it,' he said, to solemn nods from the other dads.

Failing to understand the role of testosterone in these matters, our friend stood up and suggested that a more fair approach might be to let all the children play equally.

'But then they wouldn't win,' said the father, looking half-aghast.

'Yes,' agreed our friend. 'So?'

'But what's the point in playing if you don't win?'

These were, let me remind you, six-year-olds. There isn't space here – there isn't space in this newspaper – to discuss all the things that have gone wrong with sport in America, at nearly every level, so let me just cite a few specimen examples to give you an idea of how America approaches competitive pursuits these days.

Item: In an effort to spur them on and plump up our standings in the medals tables (which is, of course, the most important thing in the universe), US swimmers were paid up to $65,000 from official sources for every medal they won at the last Olympics. Apparently, representing one's nation and doing one's best are no longer sufficient incentives.

Item: To delight the home fans and enhance their positions in the national rankings, the largest college football teams now regularly schedule matches against hopelessly inadequate opponents. In one especially proud moment for sport last season, the University of Florida, ranked number two in the nation, took on the unsung might of little Central Michigan University, and won by a score of 82 to 6.

Item: In order to watch 60 minutes of football on this year's Super Bowl on television, it was necessary to sit through 113 commercials, program trailers or product plugs. (I counted.)

Item: The average cost for a family of four to go to a Major League baseball game now is over $200.

I mention all this not to make the point that commercial overkill and blunted sportsmanship have taken much of the joy out of the sport in this country, though they have, but to explain why I love Dartmouth College basketball games so much.

Dartmouth is the local university and it is in the Ivy League, a confederation of eight venerable and brainy institutions – Harvard, Yale, Princeton, Brown, Columbia, Penn, Cornell, and Dartmouth. These kids go to Ivy League schools because they are going to become rocket scientists and professors, not because they are going to make $12 million a year playing professional basketball. They play for the love of the game, the camaraderie, the thrill of taking part – all those things we have mostly lost in this country.

I first went to a game three winters ago, when I saw a schedule in a shop window in town and noticed that the season opener was that night. I hadn't been to a basketball game in twenty years.

'Hey, Dartmouth's got a game tonight,' I announced in excitement when I got home. 'Who's coming?'

Five faces looked at me with an expression I hadn't seen since I suggested we go camping in Slovenia for our next holiday. 'Okay, I'll go on my own,' I sniffed, though in the end my youngest daughter, then eleven, took pity and accompanied me.

Well, we had a wonderful time. Dartmouth won a nail-biter, and my daughter and I came home gabbling. A few nights later, Dartmouth won another squeaker with a basket at the buzzer, and we came home gabbling again.

Now everyone wanted to come. But here's the thing. We wouldn't let them. This was our little thing.

Since then, for three seasons, going to Dartmouth games has become a ritual for my daughter and me. Everything about it is splendid. The arena where the team plays is an easy walk from our house. Tickets are cheap, and the crowds are small, friendly and loyal. An endearingly nerdy band plays perky tunes, like the theme from *Hawaii Five-O*, to get us bouncing. Afterwards, we emerge into the wintry night air and walk home chatting. It is because of these walks that I know the identities of the Spice Girls, that *Scream 2* was way cool, and that Matthew Perry is so cute it's like almost not real. When there is not the slightest chance that a living person might see, she sometimes takes my hand. It's perfect.

But at the heart of it is the game. For two hours, we shout and wince and rend our hair and become wholly absorbed with the hope that our boys can put a ball through a hoop more times than their boys. If Dartmouth win, we are elated. If they don't – well, no matter. It's just a game. This is the way sport should be.

One of the Dartmouth players last year was a seven-foot giant named Chris, who had all the attributes of greatness except, alas, an ability to play basketball. In consequence, he spent nearly the whole of his career on the low end of the bench. Very occasionally, he would be put in for the last fifteen or twenty seconds of a game. Invariably on these occasions, someone would pass him the ball and someone smaller would come and take it away. He would shake his head regretfully, then lope giraffe-like to the other end of the court. He was our favourite player.

By tradition, the last game of the season is parents' night, when parents fly in from all over to watch their sons play. Also by tradition, on the last home game, the graduating seniors are put in to start.

This particular game was of no consequence, but news of that seemed not to have reached our lanky hero. He came onto the court with an intense, psyched-up look. This was his first and last chance to shine, and he wasn't going to blow it.

He took his customary seat, cast his parents an apologetic look and watched the rest of the game through eyes welled with tears.

The referee blew the whistle to start the game. Our Chris ran
up and down the court four or five times, and then, to our dismay
and his, was taken out and returned to the bench. He had played
no more than a minute or so. He hadn't done a thing wrong –
hadn't had a chance to do a thing wrong. He took his customary
seat, cast his parents an apologetic look and watched the rest of
the game through eyes welled with tears. Someone had
forgotten to tell the coach that winning isn't everything.

This week, Dartmouth has its last home game of the season.
This year, I believe, there are two players who will be allowed to
run gamely up and down the court for a token minute or two,
and will then be replaced by abler hands.

My daughter and I have decided to skip this one. When
perfection is so difficult to find, it's hard to see it spoiled.

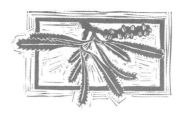

The swallow that hibernates underwater

David Quammen

'We all make our deals with life.' With this unexploded bomb of a sentence, American outdoors writer David Quammen begins the story of Gilbert White, a British naturalist of the eighteenth century, whose life was great because of what was missing from it.

What makes us human is our ability to make a choice. Gilbert White focused his life on one passion, and the loneliness that resulted never left him. Too little focus and our lives are meaningless, too much and we become warped. But read this fine writing, and I defy you not to both admire the achievement and feel the wrenching sadness of this man's life. Then have a long think about your own.

We all make our deals with life. We do it invisibly, sometimes unconsciously, and alone, without benefit of collective bargaining. We come to terms. And the terms are in every case different. Some of us hold out for more, for better, when others would settle. Some of us settle when others would hold out. We leave home, or we marry early, or we enlist, or enrol, or audition, or hunker down into a job; then we jump through the hoops, or fly off the tracks, or sell out if there happen to be buyers; we invest years, gamble dollars, marry late, light out for the territories, raise a fine family, raise hell, declare Chapter Eleven, buy a Harley-Davidson on whim and roar off down the highway clad in leather, save, scrimp, drive a fifteen-year-old Nova with rust, sacrifice joyously, piss it away, loiter, maunder, hold the course, see our child graduate, keep faith with our commitments, sow oats in a high wind, marry often, travel great distances in search of a place to call home, lose big, win big, harbor regrets, fulfil finally our wildest dream; or, alternatively, we don't. The compoundment of it all – what we've done and endured, what we've left undone and refused to endure – is our individualised deal, also called sometimes by the more august and despairing word *fate*. There is no fate. There's a lifelong balancing-off between the possible and the all-too-likely, resulting in a

> There is no fate. There's a lifelong balancing-off between the possible and the all-too-likely ...

succession of half-chosen arrangements, of which the last is burial or cremation. We can even specify that our ashes go into a silver urn, or into a mountain river. Then our deal-making is over, unless we've devised a nefariously prescriptive will. Your deal is unique to you, mine to me, but we share the process. During the early and middle decades of his adulthood, more than two centuries ago, an unassuming English clergyman named Gilbert White was arriving at a deal of his own.

This man, like you and me, had to reconcile the tension between what he might want out of life and what, on the other hand, he was willing to accept.

Gilbert White is famed as the author *of The Natural History of Selborne*, one of the most persistently cherished books in English literature. According to a recent tally, White's *Selborne* is the fourth most published title (as figured by number of different editions) in the language. White himself has been celebrated as the grandfather of ecology and as the paradigm of the natural history essayist. Despite the ponderousness of his reputation, he was in fact an exceptionally keen observer and a nifty writer. He made a great difference, at the dawn of modern science, by studying the lives and habits of animals, instead of merely their dried carcasses. He published only the one little volume, and did almost nothing else even faintly impressive, but his book is full of small insights and charm and secret significance, as potent in its own way as *Walden*.

For right now, though, let's set the book and its impact to one side. Maybe you already know *Selborne*. If not, you can read it someday in a busy airport, when you need a tranquil counterpoint to reality, and make your own judgment then. Two other facts about Gilbert White are more intriguing at the personal level – to me, anyway – than his place in literature and in science.

Fact one: He lived most of his life, and died, in the same little village where he'd been born.

Fact two: Despite 50 years of close study, he never abandoned his belief in the hibernation of swallows.

The hibernation of swallows is a misapprehension as old as Aristotle, who offered it in his *Historia Animalium* in the fourth century BC. A great number of birds 'go into hiding' rather than migrate in winter to warmer locales, according to Aristotelian pronouncement. 'Swallows, for instance, have been often found in holes, quite denuded of their feathers,' he wrote, adding that ouzels and storks and turtle doves also went torpid and hid themselves. An ouzel, that peculiar semiaquatic bird actually capable of walking on the bottom of a river, might even be imagined to hibernate underwater. A stork would presumably need a hollow tree.

There were other nuggets of erroneous biological dogma in Aristotle's work – for instance, the bit about eels being born from earthworms and earthworms being spontaneously generated in mud – but the hibernation of swallows was a fancy that endured. Two millennia later, in Gilbert White's era, the great systematising biologist Carolus Linnaeus may have believed it himself. One of Linnaeus's more conspicuous students, A. M. Berger, definitely believed it, mentioning the notion in his *Calendarium Florae* as though it were certified fact. Berger's version of swallow hibernation was the radically wrongheaded subaqueous one.

Each season had its reliable signals and early September, Berger observed, was when swallows went to hibernate underwater.

In *The Natural History of Selborne*, White cited Berger's claim, admitting that he was tempted to believe it himself. Underwater hibernation seemed to jibe with what White had noticed on his own: that swallows and their relatives, in mid-autumn, with the young fledged and the nests abandoned, tended to gather in nervous flocks around ponds and rivers. 'Did these small weak birds, some of which were nestlings twelve days ago, shift their quarters at this late season of the year to the other side of the northern tropic?' he asked. 'Or rather, is it not more probable that the next church, ruin, chalk-cliff, steep covert, or perhaps sandbank, lake or pool (as a more northern naturalist would say), may become their *hybernaculum*, and afford them a ready and obvious retreat?' This wasn't so much a rhetorical question as a genuine uncertainty within his own mind: Was it more probable, or not? He couldn't decide. *The Natural History of Selborne* took him eighteen years to compose (partly because he insisted on padding it out with a pedantic section on historical antiquities, which has been mercifully omitted from some editions), based on a long lifetime of watching and rumination. But he never did settle the question of wintering swallows.

His eyesight and his knowledge of birds pushed him towards one answer, I think, while his heart preferred another.

Selborne is a tiny, ancient village set among the hills and meadows of Hampshire, about 40 miles southwest of London. In White's time, those 40 miles represented a long journey by coach from one world to another. The lanes of Selborne are cut deep as canals by centuries of traffic and erosion. In the churchyard is a yew tree, huge in girth and guessed to have stood for perhaps more than a dozen centuries. Just beside the church is the vicarage, where Gilbert was born in 1720. His grandfather was vicar of Selborne.

In basic outline, Gilbert White's life appears simple and happy and sweet. From the age of about nine, after his grandfather's death, he was raised in a sizable house called The Wakes, just across the village green from the vicarage. He was an outdoorsy boy who planted trees and occasionally made notes on his natural history observations. He went off to boarding school, then to Oxford, and in his mid-twenties took deacon's orders, which made him essentially a licensed clergyman in search of a job. During his thirties he travelled widely around England, visiting friends and extended family, seeing the countryside, and serving in some temporary posts as a fill-in churchman.

Always, even during those years, Selborne remained his true home and retreat. In 1760, he returned there permanently. He accepted a modest clerical position nearby. He lived the rest of his life at the old family home, The Wakes. He became a serious gardener and began keeping a horticultural diary, quite terse and businesslike at first, which gradually evolved into the journal of a full-hearted naturalist. He never married or, apparently, even came close. According to a later biographer, Gilbert 'had but one mistress – Selborne'. Another scholar of White's life and work, Richard Mabey, has written: 'He never scrimped his clerical duties, but with only a few dozen marriages and burials to attend to a year, had plenty of free time to pursue his natural history.' He watched birds. He recorded the seasonal timing of their activities in his journal, year after year. He paid attention to crickets and slugs and hedgehogs and the weather and the hibernating rhythms of an old pet tortoise named Timothy. He raised cantaloupes, succulent enough to make a preacher proud. He studied the barn swallow, *Hirundo rustica*, and certain similar species (martins and swifts) with particular devotion.

Eventually he wrote his book, styling it as a series of information-filled letters to two other men, both of them naturalists better travelled and better known than he. The first edition was a modest success. Forty years after his death, the book became surprisingly, voguishly popular. Historians now talk about 'the cult of Gilbert White and Selborne'. Readers have belatedly recognised that this unprepossessing man (of whom there seems to be no surviving portrait) found great scope and great wisdom, as well as beauty and peace, within the boundaries of his little village. He lived to age 72. Needless to say, this outline leaves a hell of a lot out.

It leaves out, among other things, the tension between what he may have wanted from life and what he got.

One sample of that tension, from the larger pattern: Gilbert, unlike his grandfather, never became vicar of Selborne. He couldn't. For reasons that must have seemed adequate to a nineteen-year-old, he had gone to the wrong college at Oxford – Gilbert was an Oriel man, whereas the vicar's position at Selborne was restricted, by certain archaic regulations, to graduates of Magdalen. Disqualified to be vicar, what he eventually became instead was curate of Selborne, and the difference is more than semantic. Within the Anglican hierarchy of White's time, a curate was just a delegated assistant who functioned as acting pastor. The curacies were often short-term assignments, meagrely paid, like a non-tenure-track lectureship at a modern university. A vicar was a salaried professional; a curate, subcontracted under a vicar, was a liturgical flunky. And even the Selborne curacy came to him late in life.

Throughout most of his middle age, though he lived in Selborne, he held a curate's position, not for Selborne itself but for one or another small village in the vicinity, to which he commuted by horse. Old friends goaded him for decades: Gil, you shirking doofus, with a little push you could land a respectable Oriel vicariate somewhere else. He declined to push. At one time, when he was younger and more energised, he had tried for a good position through Oriel and been rebuffed. He wouldn't try again. He had money enough to get by. Selborne was familiar and safe, and it was home. He loved the meadows and woods. If he had any broader ambitions, they were secondary to his sense of place.

Another sample: In 1763, when Gilbert was a 42-year-old bachelor whose juices still flowed, three young sisters swept into Selborne for a summer visit and caused him some delicious perturbation. Their names were Anne, Philadelphia, and Catharine Battie. They were in their late teens and early twenties, and (as nicely said in the wonderful White biography by Richard Mabey, to which I'm indebted for most of these facts of personal history) they were 'rich, flighty and attractive. They fizzed about the village for two months, and left a perceptible dent' in Gilbert's composure. There were balls and picnics and other sorts of gently flirtatious shenanigans. Catharine was the sister who caught Gilbert's eye. Her own attention seems to have flickered more on Harry, Gilbert's much younger brother. Gilbert himself, after all, was a middle-aged man of no particular forcefulness, a bachelor past his prime, and not even a vicar but a curate. The summer interlude was fun but not serious – at least not, evidently, to the Battie sisters. They left Selborne in August. On November 1, Gilbert wrote a poem, gloomy with autumnal images and dedicated 'To the Miss Batties', which ended:

Return, blithe maidens; with you bring along
Free, native humour, all the charms of song,
The feeling heart, and unaffected ease,
Each nameless grace, and ev'ry power to please.

But they never did.

Still another sample: In 1768, White sent (indirectly, through a mutual friend) an invitation to Joseph Banks, the celebrated and wealthy young naturalist who was about to leave on a round-the-world voyage of exploration with Captain Cook. Would Mr Banks and the mutual friend care to visit Mr White in Selborne? If Banks will just do him the honour, White promised, 'he will find how many curious plants I am acquainted with in my own Country'. It must have sounded faintly pathetic. Getting no acceptance, White wrote directly to Banks, a polite but mopey letter in which he complained that, if Mr Banks and other busy colleagues wouldn't visit him, 'I must plod on by myself, with few books and no soul to communicate my doubts or discoveries to.' Joseph Banks sailed away on the *Endeavour*. He would visit Tierra del Fuego, and Tahiti, and New Zealand, and Australia (where he'd discover, among other things, kangaroos), but not Selborne.

Gilbert White was a stay-at-home guy during an age when the great naturalists made great expeditions; and he knew it. Broad travel, the collection of exotic observations and specimens, seemed fundamental to the enterprise. Linnaeus had gone to Lapland. Banks, even before the Cook voyage, had done fieldwork in Newfoundland and Labrador. Pehr Osbeck sailed to

China. Johann Gmelin got to Siberia, and Carl Peter Thunberg to Imperial Japan, eventually publishing his *Flora Japonica*. Darwin and Huxley and Hooker would later make crucial voyages of discovery. Henry Bates would bring important data and insights back from the Amazon. Alfred Russel Wallace would wander the Malay Archipelago for eight years.

Gilbert White, as he grew older, as he settled more rigidly the terms of his life, travelled less and less. Even the familiar roads of southern England got to be too much for him. By his own account, he was prone to horrible coach sickness. But we shouldn't assume that he achieved obliviousness to what he was missing.

I don't claim that these particular deprivations – of a vicar's position, of Catharine Battie's affection, of the inspiring companionship of Joseph Banks and other naturalist colleagues, of the chance to go off on a great expedition himself – were the four big facts of his life. What I suspect is that they were representative.

Swallows, like martins and swifts, feed on insects taken in flight. Their amazing agility on the wing is a prerequisite to this dietary strategy. They cruise, they dive, they swoop, they swim through the air, gathering small mouthfuls of gnat and mosquito and beetle. Aquatic insects such as mayflies and caddisflies – which emerge from the water's surface as winged adults, often in synchronous events during which one species or another fills the air with its blizzard-thick multitudes – are especially convenient food for these birds. So they tend to congregate around rivers and ponds. They are also drawn to villages and small towns, where human-made structures with overhung roofs and rafters offer good sites for their nests. But if the insect density in a certain locale isn't high, or if the insects aren't taking wing at some particular time of the year, then swallows and martins and swifts can't afford the metabolic cost of their habitual swooping and diving. They can't make a living there. So they migrate.

Besides being graceful, they have stamina. They travel long distances out of the north in order to winter in warm, buggy places. Swallows from Siberia go to Sumatra. Swallows from Canada go to South America. Swallows from Europe cross the Mediterranean and the Sahara. Although the movements of discrete populations aren't easy to track precisely, modern bird-banding work suggests that the British population *of Hirundo rustica*, the barn swallow, probably spends Christmas in South Africa.

Gilbert White never banded the birds of Selborne. Sometimes he shot them and dissected them. He peeked into their nests. Mostly he watched them, acutely but lovingly, from a respectful distance.

In *The Natural History of Selborne*, he wrote: 'The *hirundines* are a most inoffensive, harmless, entertaining, social, and useful tribe of birds: they touch no fruit in our gardens; delight, all except one species, in attaching themselves to our houses; amuse us with their migrations, songs, and marvellous agility; and clear our outlets from the annoyance of gnats and other troublesome insects.'

Then he *did* believe in swallow migration – that notably amusing attribute – as opposed to swallow hibernation? Yes and no. Elsewhere in the book, White voiced his equivocating opinion 'that, though most of the swallow kind may migrate, yet that some do stay behind and hide with us during the winter'. Joseph Banks had gone off to remote places that White would never see; the Misses Battie had gone off; so many others had gone off and left him behind – including, each autumn, most if not all of the British swallows. But maybe some of those birds lingered secretly in Selborne, mitigating the wintry isolation of a poor bachelor curate.

He imagined that they might 'lay themselves up like insects and bats, in a torpid state, to slumber away the more uncomfortable months till the return of the sun and fine weather awakens them'. Where exactly did they hide? Not in their old nests; he had checked. But he recalled the curious affinity they seemed to have for rivers and ponds, which caused him 'greatly to suspect that house-swallows have some strong attachment to water, independent of the matter of food; and though they may not retire into that element, yet they may conceal themselves in the banks of pools and rivers during the uncomfortable months of winter'.

Where were the swallows of December? He was honest enough to claim no final answer.

His book was published in 1789. He died in 1793, at his house in the village. His death came in June of the year, so we can assume that the swallows were back from Africa, nesting outside his window.

Gilbert White's reputation is based partly on the fact that he was an extraordinarily fine observer, a painstaking empiricist who relied on his own eyes and ears, not on secondhand anecdotes and theoretical preconceptions. His mistake about swallow hibernation was an uncharacteristic lapse. He had ulterior reasons, I think, for keeping the idea alive. These reasons pertain not to the ecology and behaviour of *Hirundo rustica*, of course, but to the natural history of the human soul. The swallow that hibernates underwater is a creature called yearning.

Love in the time of economic rationalism

Elliot Perlman

The traditional idea of courage in a man usually evokes images of rushing a machine-gun post, facing wild beasts or battling high seas. Risking hooves or bullets is brave, but it is also over in minutes.

There is another form of courage, the courage to endure. Often the lives of others depend not on some sudden heroic deed, but on keeping on going, day after day, and not giving up. This kind of courage does not often get recognised, yet it is all around you if you look. Equally to be found in men and women, it is probably the truest, and toughest, form of heroism there is.

We sit in the front room of a narrow house at the end of a narrow street. It is a house Frank values more than most of us value our houses. He does not own it but he had owned one once. Inside, there is an extreme austerity which gleams almost perversely. There is a faint scent of detergent. The room is sparsely furnished. Everything shines, even the carpet, thinning, like his hair. Frank values the house not merely because he waited so long to have it allocated to him but because he thinks it might just provide a semblance of normality for his children. It is his commitment to their wellbeing which keeps him going despite everything that has happened to him.

When we think of courage, we usually think of acts of altruism in the presence of great danger, acts in a time of war or in the face of some natural disaster. Acts that require this kind of courage are mostly unplanned, impulsive and of short duration.

But there is another kind of courage, the kind some people are called upon to display over protracted periods. The burden of this courage is chronic rather than acute. This kind of courage is less likely to be visible and therefore more likely to go unheralded. But the situations that elicit it are no less likely to kill, albeit to kill very slowly. It is this kind of courage that more and more men are being called upon to demonstrate in the 1990s. It is this courage that Frank displays.

If anything characterises the decade, it is the overwhelming insecurity people feel, particularly with respect to their employment. It is a feeling that is well-founded. The total number of people in Australia who are either officially unemployed or whose unemployment is less visible (those who want employment but have given up looking and those with part-time subsistence jobs who want full-time employment) is two-and-a-half million.

Is this peculiar to the 1990s? One in every three to four Australians of working age was unemployed in the 1930s. But in the Thirties, however bad things got, nobody pretended they were otherwise. Adversity was acknowledged by everybody, loudly and clearly. In the 1990s, governments and irrelevant indices on the business pages proclaim economic growth and success loudly and confidently, while in their homes, people experience hardship and suffering, silently and privately; this is what distinguishes the Nineties. The pain is ignored publicly but it is felt in the hearts of men and women in the anxious suburbs, in the stricken country towns, in the doomed factories, in the plush offices with their ducted fear and in the overcrowded crisis centres that cannot contain the flood.

There is an expectation that men should be able to provide for themselves, their partners and their children. So strong is the societal imperative to provide that most men internalise it as a personal measure of their own worth. In the absence of war, providing materially is still almost the *sine qua non* of being a man. How is one to be a man in times like these? What happens to a man in the Nineties who aspires to the security, love, family life and self-respect that the men of the previous generation took for granted? What kind of courage does it take?

Frank has two children and, were it not for them, he would not want to live. He is 42 years old.

He had served in the Navy for six years and was a qualified fitter and boiler attendant when he left. He bought a house and was working at a technical college. To keep in shape, he joined a gymnasium, which is where he met Marie.

They were married when he was 28 and she was 21. Marie became pregnant on their honeymoon. With a child coming, they needed more money. Frank took a job working night shifts at an oil refinery. It was the late 1980s and he was earning $45,000 a year. Jason was a difficult baby. He slept very little and cried a lot. Marie was having trouble coping. One morning Frank came home to find Marie very distressed. She was in tears, in her nightdress, in the dark. She confessed to having bashed their child. They had been married for eleven months.

When Alice was born a year-and-a-half later, Marie seemed more positive about being a mother. Frank thought they had largely worked it through. He was still working at the refinery, although some of his colleagues had been retrenched. That was when he started seeking solace through the church. At first, he was an irregular attender. On those occasions, Marie stayed home or went out alone. Frank was retrenched a short time later. He became a regular churchgoer after that.

Frank kept looking for another job. There weren't any. With money so short and him at home, he and Marie were arguing more. By the time he had told her that, in spite of his love for her, they were in serious trouble, Marie had already started seeing other men. Three days later, she left him, asking for nothing but her clothes. He tried to get Marie to come back but it was no use: she had no interest in him or the children. For a while, he drank more than he should and slept with women indiscriminately. He sank into depression.

He resolved that he had to get his life in order for the sake of the children. This meant cutting down on his drinking and finding work that would enable him to be with Jason and Alice: 'I want them to have a normal life. I tell them I love them every day.'

He decided to buy a milk bar. On the basis of the advice he had received from a real-estate company, he had calculated that the proceeds from the sale of his house would make it possible for him to run the milk bar and make the repayments on the property.

But Frank's home sold for less than he had been advised it would and he and the children moved into the milk bar already behind scratch. His possible salvation lay in the trade that streamed in at lunch time five days a week from the large shirt factory across the road. Three months after he started trading, the shirt factory closed. Unable to compete with cheap imports from low labour-cost countries, it moved its manufacturing offshore. Frank drowned. Yesterday, the day before I wrote this, he was declared bankrupt.

He lives with his children in a narrow house at the end of a narrow street. The house is provided by a welfare agency. There is no telephone. Clothes cannot be replaced. When he is not looking after the children, he is looking for work flexible enough for him to be there for them. But there is no work for him. He lives on a social welfare pension and assistance from the welfare agency (the funding of which is currently under threat). After a lengthy period of living in hostels, he is relieved to be in a house. He tells me he just wants his children to know they are loved. Each day he wakes to find it is all still true. Then he gets up.

If courage is that quality of character which shows itself when someone acts despite fear or lack of confidence, then it might be more prevalent among men in the Nineties than at any other time in the past 50 years. If you passed Frank on the street, you would find nothing remarkable about him. If you met his eye, he would meet yours and no doubt wish you a good day. He would probably have his children with him. He resembles neither a victim nor a hero. He looks very much like the man next to you.

The economy says

Michael Leunig

There's been a debate for years now about a new Australian flag that would reflect what we are on about as a nation. The symbol of modern Australia to me seems very obvious. Judging by our political priorities, and the forces that shape our nation, I think a large black dollar sign on a white background would just about do it. The white being for surrender.

Michael Leunig seems to feel the same way ...

THE ECONOMY SAYS

The economy says, "close the hospital"

The economy says, "build a freeway through the schoolyard"

The economy says, "cut down the forest"

The economy says, "you are all afraid of me... you are broken people... you do what I require... nothing is above me... no person can stand up to me... you are my slaves... you all run for me..."

The economy says, "build a racetrack in the park"

And then the economy says "So get stuffed; you and your values and your feelings— GET STUFFED!"

leunig

Women teaching boys

Nancy Lerner

Millions of boys today are being educated largely by women teachers. It's a vital relationship, yet it has been little studied in terms of its gender dynamics.

Recent unpublished research by Peter Downes at Cambridge indicates that four factors determine a boy's relating well to a teacher. That teacher must ideally be friendly, focused, funny and firm. Boys will only learn well from a teacher who likes them.

Nancy Lerner is a well-known US educator who writes about the classroom with clarity and passion. Yet it was late in her career that she realised she loved teaching boys. This is the story of how this discovery came about.

*O*n a May afternoon in 1994, I was waiting to meet a
group of students on the mall outside the Air and Space
Museum in Washington, DC. In the last season of my
teaching career, I had done something I had 'known' I would never
do; I had shepherded a group of teenage males on a field trip. As I
waited on the mall, orange-draped men were playing tambourines
and chanting, 'Hare Krishna', while mothers, sitting on the grass,
were feeding ice cream to small children in their laps. The sun was
shining, and I might have simply enjoyed the moment had I not felt
the overwhelming need to rush to an outdoor telephone to ask my
husband in Cleveland an urgent question.

'Allan,' I breathed, as soon as he answered. 'Is there something
wrong with a 55-year-old woman who finds such joy in the
company of fifteen-year-old boys?'

The question was rhetorical, and my husband understood exactly
what it meant. I had simply needed to 'share the ... joy'.

Yet, beneath my words lurked an unspoken question. This
was not the first time I had been surprised by the joy of teaching
in this boys' school. The question now rising to the surface was
why? ... My liberal background told me I disapproved of private
school in general and of single-sex schools for males in particular.
Therefore, when I discovered myself not only teaching in a
private boys' school, but finding it the best experience of all, I
had to ask *why*?

These *Confessions* are my attempt to answer that question ...
Is there something unexpectedly positive for women to discover
about single-sex schools for males? Since women as students
have been excluded from such schools, is there something

contradictory about the hiring of women as teachers? Or, in the absence of female students, are female teachers of special benefit? If so, is there a type of woman who is an effective teacher in an all-male school? These questions and my speculations about their answers are embedded in the narrative of my five years at a boys' school.

I was not looking for a job on the day I visited University School, a boys' school in Hunting Valley, Ohio. My job in an excellent co-ed school was secure; I loved my students, and had I wished to change, I would not have looked at a boys' school. Yet, I was intrigued by the enthusiasm of the teacher I most admired, my friend Ann Behrman, who had left her all-girls' school to chair the English Department at this boys' school.

Accepting her invitation to visit, I entered the front door to be assailed by the smell of sweat. *I could never teach here*, I thought. *It smells like a locker room!* Once upstairs in the English Office, however, I felt *never* change to *possibly*. It was not the boys who interested me then, but the men who taught them ... They shared ideas, materials and feelings; they wanted to talk about teaching. Talking with them about writing theory, I realised how hungry I had been for such collaboration. I had doubts about teaching only males, but I repressed them because I wanted to be part of that English Department.

The repressed returned with full force when I faced my first class. At my two previous schools, I had been blessed with the best and brightest students. Now I faced a class of senior English 'regulars' ... and received their first writing samples with a

The seniors assured me that things would get worse when 'Walt the Wild Man' joined the class.

sinking heart. I could only think, *What have I done to myself?* The seniors, noting my dismay, cheerfully assured me that things would get worse when 'Walt the Wild Man' joined the class.

'Why isn't Walt here now?' I asked, hoping this unknown student was busy transferring to some school in Alaska.

'He's still in drug rehabilitation,' they happily responded.

Of course, this story does have a happy ending. I never did turn those young men into great writers, but I fell in love with them – with the whole lot of them and with the daily pleasure of the classroom. For this classroom was a charged space, crackling with energy. With the text in front of them, these young men had no problem responding with spirit and intelligence and humour; I never had to work to engender discussion. The best, of course, was the rehabilitated Walt, that wild man who understood *Heart of Darkness* better than any student I knew, and who taught his peers more about the book than I did. Thinking back to my former school, I remembered one special English class which had contained more gifted boys and girls than I had seen in one room together. I also remembered that, while the students had produced extraordinary papers, they had been reluctant to engage each other in the classroom; I had not been able to spark lively discussion. I knew of no theory correlating less gifted students with more energetic discussions! Was the increased energy I was experiencing now possibly due to the all-male setting? Could the reticence of some former students be due to the presence of the opposite sex in the classroom? What could I do with this hypothesis?

What I did was to observe the same phenomenon over and over. By the next year, I was teaching Advanced Placement classes, yet it did not matter. The energy was there, whether the students were at the top or the bottom of the class. In five years of classes, I only had one that disappointed me in terms of classroom experience. Thus, I came to associate a freer and more open exchange of ideas with the all-male classroom.

Having read some of the literature about girls' schools, I knew that advocates made a similar claim for the all-female classroom. I did wonder which factor mattered more, the absence of an opposite sex or the gender of the students. I had never taught in a girls' school and had no laboratory for comparing genders, but I did have a laboratory for learning about boys. What, at least, could I discover about males together?

In a recent speech, Dr Richard Hawley, Headmaster of University School, succinctly outlined the position of those who implicitly disapprove of single-sex schooling for boys. Such people, he says:

> [base] their preferences for coeducation on the (usually unstated) assumption that males are toxic: that they are by their nature usurpers of privileges; that they are misogynist dominators; that if they are allowed to get together without any mitigating femininity, they will cause trouble.

At one time, I would certainly have been among 'such people', adding that males together not only cause trouble, but that 'the leading cause of violence is maleness'. In his book, *Boys Will Be Men*, Dr Hawley holds the 'feminist momentum' responsible for such negative images of masculinity. However, one need not be a feminist to hold such views about males or to fear that all-male schools foster unhealthy male attitudes – one need only be a reader. Over and over, classic books about boys' schools tell the same story of male competitiveness and aggression, of the power of stronger males to tyrannise weaker, of a male pack mentality that leads to bullying and to group victimisation of a scapegoat. One only has to remember that the boys killing Piggy in 'delirious abandonment' in *Lord of the Flies* are the products of a British boys' school. Or that Stephen Dedalus, at his Jesuit boys' school, is haunted by the memory of his cruel treatment by the bully Wells ... Is it any wonder that a female reader might look upon a boys' school as a breeding ground for 'toxic males'?

I certainly did not expect overt acts of brutality or violence from the males I had now engaged to teach; I did expect subtler manifestations or refined forms of the same tendencies. Did I think I was Huck Finn's Aunt Sally with some 'sivilizing' mission, or Richard Hawley's liberated feminist, waiting to apply the corrective to the problematic male? No. But I was alert to the probability that my new territory might have a different ethos ... My [new territory was] the real boys I encountered, and they told me different stories: about competitiveness, about bullying, about empowerment and identity.

Quarrelsome comradeship?

'I see you have Rich this year,' said one of my colleagues. 'My condolences. I had him as a sophomore.'

I've dubbed this student Rich because he was. His reputation as a spoiled and indulged child had preceded him. He was often absent from school when the family took off for their residence in Aspen; he was one of those kids who railed against materialism while boarding the plane. In his sophomore year, he had wanted to transfer; he just didn't feel the school was doing enough for him. Somehow, he had stayed; now, he was a senior and my prize in the draw. To my relief, I found his failure to proofread his essays the most serious charge against him. However, I did not really know him until he surprised me by signing up for a field trip to the Holocaust Museum in Washington. If he was a 'fun' kid, this wasn't a 'fun' trip and he knew it.

Of all the boys who went with me on that first trip, he was the one who seemed most profoundly moved. I remember that he sat for a very long time in a room with no exhibits, where all one could do was listen to tape-recorded voices of survivors of Auschwitz. Walking back from the museum to the hotel, I found him beside me, obviously awkward and wanting to talk.

'You know,' he said. 'When I was younger, I hated this school and wanted to leave. But now, I feel so different. You know, I would do anything for these guys in my class. I have a lot. But I would give whatever I had to help a classmate.'

'I'm glad you found good friends here,' I said, 'and I'm sure your friends know you would help them.'

'Not just my friends,' he answered. 'I would help any guy in my class. That's how I feel about the school and these guys.'

I believe that if Rich, as a freshman or sophomore, had been asked if he ought to be his brother's keeper, he would have replied, 'No way!' By the end of his senior year, though, some alchemical process had turned his baseness into gold. The same could be said of Rob, the second boy about whom I received a doom-laden forecast.

'No kid ever gave me more trouble,' said my colleague, looking at my class roster of seniors. 'He's extremely bright, but he completely ruined the class. He couldn't tolerate the lesser mortals. He wouldn't work with anyone, and he continually mustered his parents, who kept coming in complaining that he wasn't getting the education his talents deserved. He's so damned arrogant and competitive.'

Great. Just great, I thought to myself. *If he's so competitive, this class will be the clash of the Titans!* For sitting in the same class was Daniel Choi, a certified genius from Hong Kong who had only been in this country for two years. As a sophomore he had been so far ahead, I had been asked to design a separate course for him alone. I remember asking him what Shakespeare plays he had read. I'll never forget his answer. 'Well,' he said, looking down with shame. 'I haven't read *Pericles* yet.'

What will I have with the two of them? I wondered – *Gunfight at the OK Corral, academic style?*

There was no contest. Rob found himself upstaged by Daniel in every discussion, and the beauty of it was that Daniel was not even trying to compete. Thin to the point of fragility, Daniel spoke in barely audible tones. His modesty was palpably sincere.

He was simply a book lover, a knowledge-quaffer who spoke to add to the general fund of knowledge. Anyone could see that and everyone did. Even Rob. His reaction would have surprised those who had known him as a younger student. He neither exacerbated the competition, nor rallied his cohorts to confront this lone and foreign intruder, nor retreated in sullen silence. He did his best to contribute to the class and sometimes smiled in rueful but respectful acknowledgement of his second-best position. After a graduation ceremony in which Daniel walked off with all the prizes, I looked for Rob.

'You had a lot of poise up there,' I said. 'I know that without Daniel, those prizes would have been yours.'

'Don't I know it,' he replied, in rueful, genial acknowledgment.

Between sophomore and senior year, Rob had grown up. Lest I sound like Pollyanna, I can add other testimony. During Rob's freshman year at Yale, I saw his older sister and asked what he had to say about college.

'He's ecstatic,' she replied. 'He says everyone in his classes is so brilliant. He just loves it.'

The following summer I spoke to a friend, the editor of a local newspaper, who was employing Rob for the summer. 'How's he doing? I asked. 'We all love him,' she said. 'It's not just that he's so bright. He's so kind. Isn't it nice to know you produce students like that!'

Nasty peer competitiveness … was what my own map of maleness had led me to expect. And, of course, competitiveness had not disappeared. Competition pervaded the school: on the playing fields; in the listings of class honours; in the telling of SAT scores; in the plethora of contests in art, in maths, in debate; in the publishing of college acceptances. Yet in many boys, competitiveness was often superseded by another, better ethos. Some transformation could be seen by the time boys were in their senior year, which is to say, when boys were turning into men.

Normal social derision?

When Zack first entered my classroom, I easily identified him as a victim. He stuttered. At first I feared he wouldn't talk, and then I feared he would. Always thinking and wanting to challenge, he couldn't refrain from speaking, but for all his intellect and wit, his stutter was irremediable. Each time he opened his mouth, we waited – and waited – and waited for him to get the words out. Each time I feared that he would overstep some un-known boundary of his classmates' patience, and they would burst out in derision. I feared letting him go on, but I feared cutting him off more, and for the first weeks of class I experienced a squeezing of the heart every time Zack opened his mouth. The derision never came. Much later in the year, in a private meeting, he cried to me, 'You don't know how terrible it is for me. You don't know how miserable I've been.'

As I opened my mouth to offer balm for his wounds, I found myself

> As I opened my mouth to offer balm for his wounds, I found myself saying instead, 'Oh, come off it.'

saying instead, 'Oh, come off it. You've been blessed. Everyone here knows how smart you are.'

'Okay, okay,' he said, relinquishing the role of victim with a grin, then adding seriously, 'It's okay with my teachers and with the guys, but it doesn't help when I want to telephone a girl and I'm afraid I won't get the words out.'

Would Zack, whose libido was as active as his brain, have been better off in a co-ed school, in the presence of girls every day? I don't believe so; I think the presence of girls would have intimidated him into silence. In this boys' school, he had time to develop. Here, he had not been a victim. In fact, he had been protected, and he had thrived. Of course, he would be confronting girls as soon as he reached college, but perhaps, by then, he would have a better sense of himself.

Yet Zack, for all his problems, was still, recognisably, of the same species as the others. Kevin was another species altogether. It was disconcerting to talk to him, because his eyes were misaligned, and he seemed to be looking in two different directions at once. A serious student of music with ambitions to become a composer, he came from a small town in southern Ohio and boarded with a family in Cleveland in order to study at the Institute of Music. He felt he had a mission to introduce the music of Schönberg and Messiaen to boys who thought the music of the Grateful Dead was 'classical'. *A nerd*, I thought – *archetypal victim of the adolescent male!*

The first week of class, I introduced the syllabus and, having just browsed through the controversial *Black Athena*, felt compelled to explain that, while we were starting with Homer, there were elements in Egyptian culture to which the Greeks were indebted. 'We would start with Egyptian literature,' I explained, 'but there really isn't an Egyptian literature that's come down to us.'

The next day, with great courtesy, Kevin brought to class a book entitled *Egyptian Literature*. It went on that way all year. Kevin had a fund of knowledge that amazed us all. Once, when I asked a question of Scotty, a leader-of-the-pack type, he jauntily responded, 'Oh, I'll defer to Kevin on that one'. After that, *I'll defer to Kevin* became an oft-invoked formula whenever another student wished to pass the buck. Worried that Kevin was hurt or offended, I asked him privately whether he wanted me to stop the teasing.

'Oh, no,' he said. 'I'm perfectly comfortable; I know they like me.' And they did, in their own way. He never fit in; he never wanted or needed to, but he was treated by the others with respect and affection. A boys' school – the last place I would have thought good for the hyperintellectual, *unmacho* Kevin, turned out to be very good. The all-male school tolerated the eccentric student far better than the co-ed schools I had experienced ... Paradoxically, in this traditional environment, where eccentricities of hair and dress were curbed, there was space for all sorts of individual identities to emerge.

Arguing about everything

Studies have shown that many women in co-ed classrooms have '... little confidence in their own ability to speak', and that single-sex schools can be beneficial for females who 'fear failing in front of males'. In my experience, even the brightest males can fear failing in front of females. I remember Brent, a brilliant student in my class at a co-ed school, who is now a Rhodes Scholar. So often, he would remain silent all period, but come up to question or challenge me just as the bell rang.

'Brent,' I would plead, 'why don't you bring up such questions during class, so everyone could benefit from our exchange?'

'I don't know,' he would reply. I think I know; Brent was painfully shy in front of girls. It is possible that boys like Brent can benefit from single-sex schools where the style of classroom exchange has a different tenor. Certainly, I had questions and challenges from males in co-ed settings, but they were seldom as direct as the challenges I experienced from males in a single-sex setting. When Ann Behrman listed 'Things I Loved in an All-Boys' School', she noted: 'The upfrontness, the easy honesty. If a lesson wasn't flying, I knew it in 31 seconds ...'.

I knew it also. Boys demanded of me a constant integrity. If I gave an assignment whose rationale was not self-evident, I had to account for its validity if I wanted to keep their respect. When my behaviour deviated from the ideal, I was also held accountable.

I remember one especially painful class and its aftermath. College counsellors were visiting that day, and I wanted my Advanced Placement stars to shine. Instead, they became black holes. When Charlie, our existential wit, came to class late, said he was tired, and put his head down on the table, I thought I would die of humiliation. Somehow, I got through the class, but only by strutting and fretting my hour upon the stage. Looking the boys in the eye the following day, I prepared to vent my disappointment with them. Before I could open my mouth, Mike vented his disappointment with me: 'You were such a phony yesterday,' he said. 'Why were you dishing out all that bullshit?'

Poised on the brink, not knowing whether to lie by refuting the accusation or to reprimand the use of the all-too-accurate 'bullshit', I knew I had to tell the truth. 'You guys were so awful, and I was so embarrassed. I knew I was being phony, but I couldn't get out of it.'

'That's what I thought,' he said, looking around the room and nodding to the other boys as if to say, 'I told you so.'

Girls certainly would have noticed the same phoniness. However, girls would not have offered such a direct challenge. Girls probably would not have offered a challenge at all, either because they cared more about my feelings or because girls learn they must 'balance drive with deference' to succeed.

Does this make the more direct challenge a negative aspect of a boys' school? I don't think so. Certainly, some boys challenge simply for the sake of argument, because they are flexing their muscles or feeling combative. As I will discuss in the next section, challenges to new and/or insecure teachers can represent what Ann has called the more 'chilling aspects' of boys' behaviour. But I've come to associate the real challenges with the kind of scholarly discourse I most value.

In my teaching careers at coeducational schools I, like my colleagues, had received letters from appreciative students. But only from graduates of a boys' school were the letters so unexpected ... The letters were from boys I thought I had failed to reach or boys too successful to need to confess any failings. These are what I call 'Push' letters. As one boy wrote: 'When I struggled ... you pushed me to not only "get by", but to move to the next step.' A boy who had worn a smirk to class almost every day wrote from college: 'Thank you for being tough with me and fighting me. I know I never listened too well and that most of the time I resisted, but I'm glad you kept trying.' The last confession I expected was from a gifted student who had achieved a brilliant record yet wrote: 'I never bluffed so much in front of teachers as before you ... You taught me to understand works that I previously read for showing off. I thought it might be good for me to make you realise how much I have changed ...'

It is almost as if, in high school, these boys had occupied one self while hovering nearby was an avatar they either did not recognise or could not occupy. Nor could they yet recognise that the push into that other self had not come from me.

Males have their own identity problems. If a girl's sense of herself may flourish through single-sex education, the corollary should not be that a boy must be deprived of that potential. In education, we are talking neither about adults nor about quantities of power, but about the development of human beings. Yet boys are not perceived as needy. Perhaps that is because common wisdom tells us that even if males are insecure, they cannot talk about their problems ... Indeed, one finding of the Gilligan and Phelps' 1988 report on boys at Middlesex School (founded as a boys' school but now co-ed) was that 'males were significantly less likely than females to share negative self-feelings with others'.

Teaching at co-ed schools, I found this image of the adolescent male valid; teaching at a boys' school, I often found it invalid.

I was teaching at a boys' school and, uncharacteristically, two of my best students walked in fifteen minutes late.

'Okay,' I asked, 'what is it?' noting their downcast looks and wondering if I was setting myself up for some outrageous answer.

'Sorry,' they groaned, with no attempt at bravado. 'We were on the telephone [with the local girls' school]. We're so miserable. Can you tell us why girls are so mean to us? We got dumped over the weekend.'

Surprised, I looked around the room to see if such an admission of *macho*-failure would elicit derision from the other boys. I was even more surprised to see many of them nod in recognition and sympathy ... Over and over during my five years, I witnessed boys admitting their vulnerabilities in front of other boys, revealing intimate details about everything from physical or emotional illness to problems with their dysfunctional families. Sometimes they were so naked in their admissions, I wished the stereotype of the repressed male were truer. I remember one boy who couldn't answer a routine question on *The Odyssey*. I expected no major humiliation; he simply hadn't done the reading. But before I could move on he blurted out, 'I know I'm dumb. I'm the dumb one in the family. My father keeps telling me that.'

Revelations ran rampant during try-outs for the junior speech contest or in assembly during senior speeches. Have boys changed from the way they were in 1988, when Ann taught in this boys' school and Gilligan and Phelps published their study? ... Two of the most serious speeches given in school assembly dispelled entirely the myth of male reticence. In one, a student discussed his struggle with clinical depression; in the other, a student discussed his struggle with Crohn's Disease, detailing his bowel movements as evidence. It is hard to know whether this phenomenon is merely a fad or a somewhat unruly but healthy aspect of a male's emerging identity. If it is healthy, we ought to ask whether it is happening everywhere or whether the all-male setting provides a better environment for males to work out their problems. It seemed to me that boys might be seeking compassion rather than competition from each other.

Yet I had to consider other interpretations ... Carol Pribble, drama director and teacher, says that students tell her they prefer discussing their problems with women teachers: 'They see women as people who are willing to sit down and think through a problem and men as people who will more likely give them a quick response.'

This statement leads me to some logical propositions: If boys are now expressing painful feelings they otherwise might have repressed; if they are turning more often to women than to men for help; then the role of women in a boys' school may be crucial. This ... is to suggest that administrators of boys' schools should look upon the hiring of women not as something good in the abstract or as compliance with mandates from overseeing agencies, but as a way of meeting the real needs of real boys.

The female teacher in the all-male school

When Ann Behrman first suggested I might like teaching at a boys' school, I had a somewhat hostile reaction: 'Why would I abandon the teaching of young women to teach a bunch of boys?' I asked.

'Because they need women to teach them,' she replied, and I read into the words 'teach them' more than just the teaching of literature ... From the moment I began teaching in a boys' school,

I could see how boys … did gravitate towards women on the faculty and staff. You could see them in groups, chatting with the receptionist, lining up outside the office of the only female Dean, chatting with the secretary of the athletic office. What astonished me was the ease and comfort I felt with whatever boys were 'hanging around' me at any moment. What was obvious was that they were looking to women for friendship, for someone to talk to, for someone to tell their troubles to.

To be fair though, they were also hanging around the male maths teacher – who always had boys piled up two and three deep in his office. There were always African-American students hanging around the white male teacher in charge of the 'Cultural Awareness' Society, and computer nerds hanging around the teacher who taught computer. They hung around anyone in whom they sensed an openness or from whom they caught a whiff of benevolence toward adolescents. A female colleague told me, 'A couple of boys have sobbed in my arms when things have gotten bad …' But a male colleague told me about a student I regarded as cold and self-contained: 'I can tell you that he has cried his heart out to me.'

Thus I cannot say definitively that boys turn more to women than to men for help or that men demonstrate less capacity for sympathetic response. Yet my strong sense is that many boys wanted and needed adult women in their environment; they responded to women with openness, generosity, and a chivalry that indicated a touching (if anachronistic) awareness of the gender difference …

The one time I was certain being female had a significant impact, I turned out to be wrong. My senior class had tackled Aeschylus' *Agamemnon*, and we had paid close attention to the sexual imagery marking the antagonism between Agamemnon and Clytemnestra. After class, Steve asked me if I would mind reading a short story he had been working on – one having nothing to do with the class. The story was blatantly erotic, virtually pornographic. I felt tricked, offended, appalled. *Just because I am a woman discussing sexual imagery in literature, he thinks he can get away with this trash*, I thought – until I discovered that he had given the story to the Headmaster and to another male teacher. He thought of himself as a writer and he wanted several opinions; he did not seem to be distinguishing me as a woman who might react differently. Even in discussing such intimate details, Steve and his peers seemed to feel as comfortable with female as with male teachers.

However, that ease of relationship between the boys and women around middle age was replaced by tension when the boys encountered women closer to their own age.

I had learnt that the boys could, indeed, be brutal towards young, inexperienced teachers in general. During my five years, two young female teachers left the school with bitter feelings about their treatment by the boys. One was a woman whose training was in English but who, for some reason, had been hired to teach biology, a field in which she had insufficient training. Another was a radical feminist who felt she had a duty to indoctrinate the boys and could be overheard telling them to 'sit down, shut up, and don't speak until I tell you to'. It seemed obvious to me that our boys needed to extend some humane understanding to new teachers in general. It also seemed obvious that these teachers were not well-prepared for teaching; however, my younger male colleagues felt our boys deserved the label of 'male chauvinists' and were woefully unprepared for the real world of women.

Their point of view seemed to be borne out in the next year when three young woman came as teaching interns. Several of us, as older faculty women, were now more alert to the need to help younger women.

We were thus more prepared to handle problems when the female Dean of Students reported to us that two of the young women were too casual and even flirtatious with students. At an all-female dinner, we gave them time to vent their feelings, and they were very angry at some of the boys who had made inappropriate remarks to them. 'This is such a male-dominated school,' one of the women insisted. There was no question that the students' behaviour had been inappropriate, but the young women seemed unaware of their own role in provoking such behaviour. Nor did they recognise their obligation as teachers to educate rather than to vent their anger. Experienced teachers know that moments of conflict are also great teaching moments, but these were not experienced teachers. The opportunity was there to teach the boys something about women in the world today, but it was missed. Instead, the boys were reprimanded by male authorities.

This experience does suggest that the presence of young women is problematic. If boys are in an all-male setting to avoid the distraction of the opposite sex, then the effect of introducing young women is catalytic. Does that mean that young women teachers should be avoided?

Certainly not. I think it is vitally important that young women teachers join the faculties of all-male schools, but it is foolish to think that they should not be chosen with special care. A young woman who is really competent in her field and secure in her identity has a unique teaching opportunity in the all-male environment. One of my colleagues provides a case in point.

Jannie Brown, 25 years old with a Master's degree from Georgetown University, was hired at the same time as I. Meeting her for the first time at a faculty party, my husband surprised me with this question:

'They're not really going to let her teach in a boys' school, are they?'

'What could you possibly mean? She's great. She'll be a wonderful teacher.'

'Nancy, have you looked at her?'

'Of course I've looked at her. She's very cute.'

'Well, you haven't looked at her as those boys are going to look at her. You've never been a teenage male.'

He was right about that. And he was right about the way they looked at Jannie. In a moment of marvellous candour, one of my students once told me, 'Dr Lerner, if you really knew what went on in our minds, you'd never speak to us again.'

'Fortunately for you,' I replied, 'I don't know.' But I found out. During that first year, Jannie received several messages from the boys including

> 'Dr Lerner, if you really knew what went on in our minds, you'd never speak to us again.'

letters professing both love and lust. The male teachers in our department informed us that the walls of the boys' lavatory were covered with some very crude messages for her. Yet the experience was positive in several ways.

Jannie's presence in the school provided the antidote to the negative experience of the other young women mentioned above. Having grown up in a family of three brothers, she was neither offended nor surprised at the reactions of adolescent males to females. She knew how to maintain the boundaries between teacher and student; if a student's behaviour towards her was inappropriate, she let him know that he had overstepped the bounds without demolishing him in the process. Above all, she was a competent and gifted teacher. She knew her stuff, and I believe that competence was the strongest factor in making her presence beneficial for her students. They knew they were getting a good education in her English classroom.

They were also getting a good education about women. When Jannie became pregnant, she continued teaching up until the time her baby was born – three weeks early, right before spring final exams. Their awareness of her changing body, their concern for her when she was confined to three weeks of bed rest lest she miscarry, her openness in sharing her feelings, taught them a great deal. Both male and female teachers use Toni Morrison's *Beloved* in the junior English curriculum. Teaching a novel whose most dramatic scene occurs when a slave owner beats a pregnant woman, Jannie was a living embodiment of a pregnant woman's feelings. The boys were richer because she brought a woman's perspective to their experience of the novel. In terms of their education for life experiences, they were also richer because she shared with them the difficult decision to leave a profession she loved to be a full-time mother.

If a boys' school hopes to challenge the criticisms of privilege, isolation from the 'real world' and the perpetuation of misogyny, then some attention must be paid to the way women are perceived in the school environment. The quality of environment is also a factor if the boys' schools hope to attract strong and talented teachers.

What, then, can I and the colleagues whose thoughts inform these *Confessions* say to women? Women teachers might be good for boys, but would a boys' school be good for women? For one thing, they might find their own stereotypes about males fruitfully challenged. For another, they might discover the joy I experienced on that trip to Washington with students. So let me end where I began …

I had never planned to take that trip. However, because I gave a school-wide presentation about the Holocaust Museum, I felt compelled to offer to take any interested boys who wished to visit the Museum. I hardly expected that any would want to spend a spring weekend viewing photos and artifacts from the concentration camps. Yet, so many students signed up that I had to arrange two different trips … Arriving on a Saturday morning, we spent a long and obviously painful afternoon at the Museum; after dinner, the boys were free for certain activities with the understanding that they had to check in with me personally at the hotel by midnight. At exactly midnight, one group of four knocked on my hotel door, told me they were reporting in, then lingered in the doorway, some of them commenting on the day. They stood there so long I finally asked if they wanted to come in for a moment to talk.

I don't think they left until 3 a.m. They sat on chairs or on the floor and talked about everything that philosophically minded people have ever talked about: the nature of evil, the existence of God, the possibility of progress, their own writing and poetry and what else I don't even remember. All I remember was the joy of the experience. They were my friends. They were my colleagues. They were alive and sensitive and concerned and, for the space of that time at least, they healed that malady of cynicism that inhabited my soul.

But part of the amazement was also that, at moments, I remembered with a shock who I was and who they were: that I was born before television, while they were downloading satellite images onto their computers; that I knew nothing of being an adolescent male in the 1990s; and, especially, that I was female and they were male. Yet I felt a sense of absolute oneness with them …

The value of women teaching in a boys' school is that the awareness of the differences allows us to feel the joy of transcending them.

No sweet dreams in the small hours

Bob Ellis

As we reach the middle of our own lives, our parents' age and frailty grasps our attention and concern. This is a ferociously honest, detailed and thoughtful piece. Bob Ellis is a man who seems to think and live from his guts, and you can feel those guts churning in these lines, as he grapples with his mother's fragility in her advancing years.

Many old people would, I think, wish for offspring who cared this intensely.

My mother Elsie turns 87 this week. She's home again after spending the best part of three months in different hospitals, one of them far from all her living friends (though a dead one, Gladys, lived and lately died a few streets from it), and my sister Kay and I are tending her now. At home. And sleeping interrupted sleeps in the unchanged bedrooms of our childhood. And grappling with big decisions.

Elsie's trouble, not uncommon, is unruly blood pressure and, about 4 a.m. sometimes, a wildly racing heart. (I know now why most old people die at 4 or 5 a.m., unpeacefully, in their sleep. They die of bad dreams – a surging heart, a stroke, a sudden swift quietus – for the dreams, and some have Death in them, or the Devil, are harrowingly real.) These things, and the maladroit drug mixtures pushed at her condition by overworked doctors, and doled out, sometimes, by weary nurses in the wrong proportions – or so it is said, as the prescriptions vary. My vigilant sister saved her life more than once last week, or so she believed, correcting the dose.

It would all be easier if she was a vegetable or a babbling old fool. We could let her go then, or let conventional medicine do its merciful worst. But her mind is fine, her memory clear, and her conversation keen. She can walk, with difficulty with her two new hips, on a walking frame. And she is afraid, deeply afraid, of dying. If there are no atheists in foxholes, there are likewise few, very few, resurrectionists now aged 87 in terminal wards. They have seen too much of things. They know how it happens. And Elsie has been alone at night in an empty house of old memories for ten years now, and she can't abide it any more.

And this is our mother, and we don't know what to do.

A nursing home, for various reasons, not least John Howard's innumerate confusions but mainly the horror (waking at night in an unfamiliar room to hear the cries of the mad), is out, or probably out. So, too, in the end, though with misgivings, is the option of sharing her last years between us – in Yarrawonga, almost 1300 kilometres from all her friends and known places, and in Sydney, 800 kilometres away. And rebuilding our houses, I guess, with ramps and handrails, so she can totter about, get up in the night without falling down. These are the choices you make when you go as a student away from your country town and choose, for whatever cause, not to come back, across those famous tyrannies of distance that sever us all from love and home. And the childhood bedrooms we should have slept in more often. And the backyards we should sit in, quietly thinking, and looking out at a view of the town.

... this is our mother, and we don't know what to do.

We'll work it out, I suppose, with a roster of neighbours, paid or not, who sleep over one night a week, and a paid nurse maybe two nights, or a 50-year-old student maybe two nights, and frequent visits, a week or two at a time, from Kay and me and our children and spouses and nieces. There will be ways, oh yes indeed, there will be ways of seeing her out.

We'll get her a lot of talking books, because reading is harder now. And satellite television, thank heaven (literally), is accessible in Lismore, with twenty channels at all hours to prattle her back to sleep, old movies, documentaries, *I Love Lucy*. And she can call her surviving friends on the phone and earnestly talk by the hour of those lesser things that old girls talk of. The heat. The grandchildren's prospects. The murderers of Princess Di. And we will talk to her, too, at all hours.

And this is adequate, I suppose. This is fair enough, on the crumbling final edge of a good innings, of a life that saw and survived a remarkable century. This is fair enough, I suppose. These are her dues.

But doubts form, and thoughts flow, especially about 4 a.m., when I sit and write these fumbling words to myself in the dark.

One of them, one of the thoughts, is how seriously wrong we all have been in following the fashions of this century. Having smaller families. Pursuing careers across thousands of miles – and a fruitless goal of self-esteem that soon, in a moment, is gone, is a mocking void. In the old world, we would have stayed home and lived a few blocks away, and our five or seven or fourteen children would have called in on their grandmother once a week – and on their grandfather Keith, when he lived. And our bloodline, our clan, would have kept its most primal thing, its address. Its own native country. And Elsie would not now lie awake in a long-loved room, in an empty house, in her 88th year, with a single earphone hearing a stranger reading a book, and waiting for the dawn. That, or the final fibrillation, whichever comes first.

This reasoning is flawed, of course, for to do it would mean not having met my wife, nor Kay her husband, nor those pleasures of travel across the world that we both have had. Yet a lot of what we learnt there – in Ireland, Eritrea, Nepal, Samoa, New Zealand – is mostly what I am saying: that family matters, and it must be better served. In some good places, it is, but not here, not now. For we have outgrown the goodness of our forefathers. We have learnt, and learnt with great skill and long practice, how not to care. We have learnt that everyone is expendable, parents too. We have learnt to make money. We have learnt to cope.

And the work isn't there anyway, in Lismore, we argue. Kids have to go away now to seek work as I did, or lose the dole. One job listed by the Lismore CES is for a young female. In a massage parlour. In Melbourne. Go seek it, girlie, the message is, or lose the dole. Go quickly, go now. So my kids will stay, for better or worse, in the city. And my mum will die in the country, alone.

I will write a book soon, I have promised myself, called *An Etiquette For the Dying* – on how to behave on your deathbed and by the deathbeds of others. It will contain some things I have learnt from Elsie and Keith and John Hepworth, the writer, and Francis James, my great eccentric hero, about that ultimate challenge of mannerly grace when time is so short and the visitors crowd with smiles and falsehoods and lame good cheer. We have much to learn of these matters, I think, in this jaded, agnostic age. We have to learn, above all, how not to lie, and yet to be kind. And this is hard.

And I wish my mother Elsie well. And I wish her, in her final extremity, a final certitude of love. And I wish her, however dim and shallow it might seem, a happy birthday.

Good on you, Mum. Sleep well.

Home from the mine

Bill Brandt

My twenty years of work with families in trouble has given me a huge respect for the way some men and women work together under pressure. Lately, history has been revised to give the impression that men and women do not get along, that romantic love is a modern (and false) invention, that male–female relationships are in fact intrinsically oppressive.

I grew up in the part of England where this photo was taken. I even recognise the wallpaper. It evokes many memories. Perhaps this is why I see great tenderness and mutual sacrifice in this image. I think the capacity for teamwork is part of the human legacy and has a glory all of its own. If we know this is possible under the terrible circumstances of the industrial revolution, it heartens us that we might aim as high.

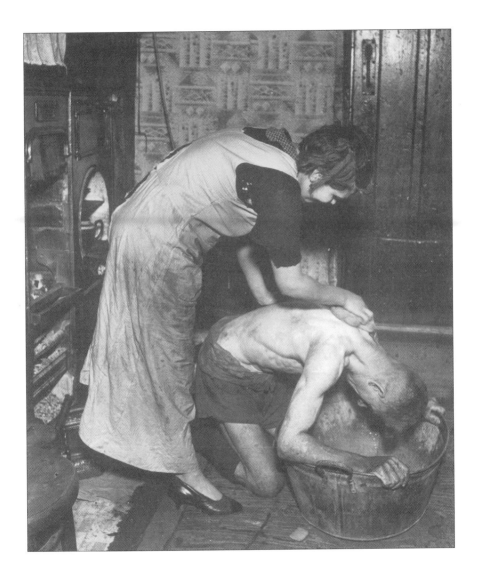

The last time I hit a woman

Adam Mitchell

Adam Mitchell grew up in a home where the irrational rages of his mother went unopposed, because his father believed women needed special understanding.

As he moved into the bigger world, he found this belief system seemed to fit the facts there, too.

Part 1

I will never forget the intensity and range of emotions I experienced the last time that I hit a woman.

I know now, as I knew then, that it doesn't matter:

That she had attacked me first, verbally and emotionally;

That she was the first to begin shouting and intimidating;

That she was much bigger and much stronger than I;

That she hit me first; or

That I only hit her once, with an open hand rather than with a clenched fist, and that my blow probably struck her on the arm though she had hit me in the face with great force.

I remember immediately feeling intense shame for what I had done. And I remember feeling very anxious. I loved that woman very much and I was dependant on her love and care. I remember the terrifying dread that went with the thought that she would withdraw her love completely because of what I had done, that she might even abandon me because of my violence.

I remember the shocked look on her face. It was the first time I had hit her in spite of her many provocations during previous arguments, and in spite of her other acts of violence toward me.

I knew that I had crossed a line and that it would be very difficult, and perhaps impossible, to ever return to the other side.

And then she said the words that I most feared hearing: 'You go to your room and stay there until your father comes home!'

I was only seven years old at the time and I had struck my mother.

I sat in my room for hours, waiting anxiously. I did not think that my father would hit me because of what I had done to my mother. I expected that he and I would talk through what had happened, and I knew that I could not defend or justify what I had done.

I was anxious because I could not think of a way to resolve the situation which had developed and because I could not think of a way to effectively make amends.

I also knew that my mother would probably be expecting him to physically punish me and that she would be pressuring him to 'teach me a lesson I would never forget'. But I trusted my father to be fair and reasonable, and not to use violence to try to teach me not to be violent.

What I feared most about the conversation I would have with my father was that I would have lost his respect because of what I had done. And, even at the age of seven, it was very important to me to be respected and loved by both of my parents, and my mother's love and respect had always been very conditional, even before I had hit her this one and only time.

My father came to my room soon after he arrived home from work. We talked. We reasoned. We analysed.

One outcome of our long talk was that I never hit my mother again, in spite of ongoing and repeated provocations, and I have also never hit any other woman.

My father did not attempt to shame me for my part in what had happened. My father did not attempt to intimidate me or terrorise me.

My father talked with me about his view of the differences between men and women. And, because much of what he told me does not conform to politically correct thinking, I will not report all of what we discussed.

I will relate the part of our conversation which dealt with what I would have to do to resolve the situation that had developed.

He made it clear that I would have to apologise to my mother for hitting her. I already knew that, but I wanted to know if she would have to apologise to me for hitting me.

My father explained that the world requires only men to be responsible and accountable for their thoughts, their feelings and their actions. Women, he suggested, are always permitted to blame others for what they think and feel and do. My mother, he explained, would maintain her belief that I had 'made' her hit me first and would insist that I needed to change so that she wouldn't 'have to yell' at me or hit me ever again.

> Women, he suggested, are always permitted to blame others for what they think and feel and do.

I remember saying that I did not think that was fair. My father explained that fairness is a male value which most women do not understand or appreciate.

During my apology to my mother, as my father had predicted, she demanded that I acknowledge that I had caused her to hit me, that her violence was my fault. My father had advised me not to argue the point, even though, objectively speaking, it was not true.

He explained I could use logic and rationality to devise an acceptable response to her demand without having to lie to her by falsely admitting that I thought her violence was my fault. He advised me to keep my logic to myself, explaining that women do not highly value logic at the best of times and that they detest it when they are emotionally upset. (I told you that much of our discussion was not politically correct.)

Knowing that I had not been responsible for her violence and that, except in very special circumstances, I could not be responsible for any future acts of violence she might commit against me, I was told that it was acceptable for me to promise: 'I will never again do anything which will cause you to hit me'.

My mother seemed to infer that this promise contained some acknowledgment that I felt responsible for what had already occurred. After telling me how much I had disappointed her, and after telling me what a 'bad little boy' I had been, she allowed that I might one day again earn her respect and her trust.

My father then bore the brunt of her unresolved rage. That night she threatened to leave him because she thought he should have disciplined me physically and that he had let me off too easily.

Part 2

In my life, I have found that my father's politically incorrect perspective does not only apply to intimate relationships.

I remember an incident with a teacher when I was eleven years old. My female maths teacher had graded a test the whole class had taken and had distributed our test papers with our scores. It was a twenty-question test.

My grade was 95 percent. It appeared that I had got one of the answers wrong.

I was a child prodigy in maths and it was unusual for me to get a wrong answer when doing tests with students my own age. I rechecked the answer that had been marked wrong. I found that my answer was correct.

I brought this to the attention of the teacher. I asked her to regrade my paper and credit me with a score of 100 percent. She checked her answer sheet and it showed an answer different to mine. I said that the answer sheet had to be wrong and that I would do the problem on the blackboard to show why my answer was correct.

She flew into a rage. She started yelling at me in front of the class and attacked me for even suggesting that the answer sheet could possibly be wrong. She said that every teacher who used the same textbook would be using the same answer sheets we were using, and that 'they' would never allow an error on an answer sheet which is so widely used in schools.

I calmly offered again to do the problem on the blackboard so that I could show the correct answer.

Then, to my amazement, she began to argue that there could be more than one correct answer to a maths problem and that the answer given on the answer sheet was probably more correct than the answer I had got.

We were working with numerical calculations, not with the maths of quantum physics, and I told her there was only one correct answer in this case and that it was different to what was shown on the answer sheet. I offered again to work it out on the board.

Her response was to send me to the principal's office for discipline.

As fate would have it, this particular principal was a gifted maths teacher. He allowed me to do the problem on paper and acknowledged that my answer was correct and that the answer given on the answer sheet was incorrect.

He and I agreed that many students would have been given a grade five percent lower than the grade they had earned.

He then explained to me that he was not going to require, or even ask, the teacher to regrade the test papers. He said that the rightness or wrongness of the answer had now become a side issue and that the central issue was that I had challenged the authority of the teacher in the classroom.

I would be required to apologise to the teacher for disrupting her class. No mention was to be made of the correct answer to the disputed question. If I did not want to apologise, I would be suspended from school and would only be allowed to return when I was ready to apologise unconditionally.

This betrayal by a trusted, adult male was a valuable and important lesson for me. As well as being a maths teacher, the principal was the coach of the school football team and a referee for senior football matches involving other schools in our region. I still think that he should have had a better understanding of what constitutes fairness and objectivity in resolving disputes.

He had his own problems. He had to supervise and support a female maths teacher who, unlike the many competent female maths teachers I have known, did not actually understand maths.

It was the first time in my life I had witnessed a man in a position of authority willingly disregarding matters of fact in order to take a position favourable to a female in a subordinate position.

Although he had acknowledged that the answer on the answer sheet was incorrect, he was wholly unwilling to acknowledge the greater error. For him, a five percent error on just one maths test – which would corrupt the scores of both male and female students equally – was unimportant when compared with the need of the teacher to maintain control in her classroom. He actively reinforced her determination to remain in error at the expense of all her students: an acknowledgment that I had been right might undermine the other students' confidence in the teacher.

I cannot say that he would not have done the same thing to protect an incompetent male maths teacher. It may or may not have been a gender issue. It is, however, a pattern of behaviour I have observed in many males when gender is a possible factor in disputes in which they are asked or required to mediate.

Part 3

In spite of lessons learnt early in my life, I still managed to marry a woman who, during our ten years together, was frequently violent, both emotionally and physically. I never responded to her violence by becoming violent myself. As I stated near the beginning of this, I have not hit a woman since I was seven years old.

When I finally accepted that my partner was not going to acknowledge that her violence was a problem, and that she was not going to make any efforts to change, I left the marriage.

During the 'sorting out' process over the next several months, we disagreed about something and she flew into a rage. She made a comment which helped me finalise the distancing process. She screamed:

'I have never forgiven you for the way you looked at me the first time I hit you.'

'How did I look?' I asked.

'You looked hurt and shocked and angry and disgusted.'

'How should I have looked after you hit me?' I asked.

'I needed for you to understand how I was feeling at that time. I needed your support, not your anger,' she said.

I understood then why she had never apologised for that act of violence or for any of her many other violent assaults. She never knew that she had a problem. No-one could tell her that she had a problem. No-one could help her with a problem she did not know about and could not be told about.

There are very few programs for women who act violently, and very little acknowledgment of the extent of women's violence. I didn't realise the extent of women's violence until I started coming to terms with my own experiences, and began to read more of the research on the subject. I was certainly aware of all the attention and publicity given to male violence. As a result of this unbalanced presentation of domestic violence, like many males who have been in relationships with violence-prone women, I thought I was an exception to the rule. Like most males who experience women's violence, I did not report her behaviour to anyone, officially or unofficially.

A vast proportion of women's violence towards men is not reported, except to researchers, who ask in an environment which protects many women from any immediate consequences resulting from their behaviour. In those situations, both men and women admit the extent to which women perpetrate violence in relationships.

Results from research projects of this type need to be acknowledged in any program aiming to teach adolescent males about violence. Many of those males will also want to learn how their mothers can be helped to be less violent.

The rites of manhood

Alden Nowlan

Young women are a real problem for us as young men, because they can make us so happy it almost prevents logical thought. The risk, then, is that we become so lost in this intoxication that we don't see them as people at all.

In this poem, a young man out on the town is set in his mind on what a young woman can give him – only to find that she has needs and frailties, too. His conscience seizes him, and he begins to learn one of life's most important lessons.

Alden Nowlan was probably Canada's best-known poet of the twentieth century.

It's snowing hard enough that the taxis aren't running
I'm walking home, my night's work finished,
long after midnight, with the whole city to myself,
when across the street I see a very young American sailor
standing over a girl who's kneeling on the sidewalk
and refuses to get up although he's yelling at her
to tell him where she lives so he can take her there
before they both freeze. The pair of them are drunk
and my guess is he picked her up in a bar
and later they got separated from his buddies
and at first it was great fun to play at being
an old salt at liberty in a port full of women with
hinges on their heels, but by now he wants only to
find a solution to the infinitely complex
problem of what to do about her before he falls into
the hands of the police or the shore patrol
– and what keeps this from being squalid is
what's happening to him inside:
if there were other sailors here
it would be possible for him
to abandon her where she is and joke about it
later, but he's alone and the guilt can't be
divided into small forgettable pieces;
he's finding out what it means
to be a man and how different it is
from the way that only hours ago he imagined it.

The long goodbye

Simon McCulloch

I've known Simon for years. He has always been truthful, open and not one to conform or fit in.

When I heard he had moved to Flinders Island to build a cabin and care for his ageing father who suffered from Alzheimer's disease, I knew he would be breaking new ground both for himself and for men everywhere. In fact, Simon found himself wondering, 'Was this a man thing to do?'

These are some extracts from his diary, a few months into this phase of his life. The writing is raw, real and instructive.

Maybe the beginning was as a young boy. I'm not sure. To have time with my father was an important 'wanting'. I never did get that time. I don't remember thinking, *I want time to be with Dad*, or anything like that. I just remember time with Dad had some sense of adventure, of the unknown.

Even as I write this, I don't think that what we are doing now somehow comes close to those feelings and wants I had as a young boy. Here we both are, on an island in the middle of Bass Strait. It is an adventure, a lot of situations are new. We have to be resourceful. If I stand back and look at us, I'm the father and he is the son. I'm responsible for nearly everything. I'm learning to enjoy the experience, to relax.

Learning not to feel guilty about getting a carer's pension and not having a job. Though I have not worked so constantly and sometimes so hard at any other time in my life. Taking charge of someone else's life and trying to maintain some freedom, or some consensus for my father - it's hard. There has to be endless patience, which I don't have.

To write about myself living on an island with my father ... God knows the whole reason why I'm doing such a thing. Is this a man thing to do? I don't hear of other men doing it. I think fathers have skills they can pass on to their children; my mother passed on her skills to me, but my father didn't teach me anything of his skills - music,

> Is this a man thing to do? I don't hear of other men doing it.

writing poetry, carpentry. I've been taught bloody-mindedness and indifference.

This is very disjointed at the moment. I want to write what moves me to choose to do this adventure with my dad. Since I was eleven years old, I have wanted my father to take me on holidays with him. You see, he used to go away walking for two weeks every year. My mother would kick him out of the house. He always promised to take me with him the next time, but he never did. So now it seems as though I'm taking my father away and having adventures. Two big kids having a midlife, and late-life, dad-and-son thing. But this man I'm with is not the man I knew as my father. This man does not know where he is, he cannot remember where he sleeps, if he has been discharged from the army (1946). He knows he is losing his hold on reality, and he says, 'I just need to get orientated to what is happening'. He hopes that he will fall asleep and when he wakes, everything will be clear and he will know! I feel for him: it's a bit like recovering from an anaesthetic, trying to get the mind to unclog, to stop everything from escaping so he can remember his place in his book of life.

I took my father into my home towards the end of 1997; my mother had died in 1996, in July. He has Alzheimer's. For a while, Dad was in an old folks' home. I watched as he became more detached and distant. I even think he began to shrink. We combined what we had and built a house of tin (red) on Flinders Island. It's not finished yet; we call it the Red Shed.

Diary entry, some time in mid-1998: One of a few bitter moments. There was probably, once, a time when my father could have changed the way he felt about people, himself and the world. In his uncaring moments, when his hatred and anger could not be suppressed, and he muttered his vitriolic remarks, his poisonous statements, his cruel and vicious taunts, there may have been a way to pause, and reflect the damage he was doing to himself, his wife, his family. Now it may be too late, because the mind that may have helped has rebelled and is closing its doors. He may be stuck with his patronising attitude, his persistent lies, and his never-ending stubborn anger and hatred. Outwardly, to others in the world, he seems a sweet, polite, nice old man. The charming man.

This relationship I have with him is one of the most unhealthy I have been involved in. I feel hopeless, and helpless. There is no sense of joy, peace, contentment. Every day is a chore. I'm not sure why I took on the task of looking after my father. I mean, I can come up with all those noble statements like 'I could not handle seeing him in a home' or 'He's my father and I love him.' But right now, I don't like him. He is impossible to get close to, he lies all the time. He can't give a straight answer ever. He is a loner who can't stay away from people. There are times when I hate him so much. He is always so distant, nothing intimate or loving about him at all.

One of the most wearing aspects of this relationship is the stubbornness. It is all-encompassing, pervasive, insurmountable, unswerving. It kills everything positive. It nurtures pain, hardship, misery; it keeps pain lingering on and on. Psychological torture, executed with the finesse of a surgeon using a very sharp scalpel. There is no let-up; there appear to be moments of respite, but always underlying the false calm and peace is the wicked and calculating comment, needle-thin, blade-sharp, and deadly accurate in its placement. For my father, every moment of wakefulness is a rich source and armoury of spite, dislike, put-down and self-loathing.

I think that I am going to end up just like him. My dad has not been able to accept that my mother is dead. Over the last two years, I have on many occasions told him that she is dead. But he is unable to comprehend her death. He still thinks she is around and will turn up, or that she is off with some other bloke who has a bigger dick than he has. Dad is deeply paranoid, thinking the world is full of people and situations that are out to get him, do him down or harm him.

I know that if I put myself in my father's place, I would feel lost, depressed, lonely, sad, frightened, unloved, pissed-off, angry, helpless. I don't know anyone, who I am, where I am.

I am moving into a new region for living with what is happening in my life. The depression is infectious. I took the plunge and now we are both on antidepressants. I think it is working. Certainly, Dad is a lot calmer, or maybe I am – who knows? I feel better; I have started work at finishing the house. It always seems so much hard work. I have to continually watch out for Dad, who has a habit of taking off on his own. The other day, he disappeared. He had gone looking for the dog who had also wandered off (male dog, mind you). So I alerted the cops after two hours of looking, told them not to come until I had checked the whole area. Meanwhile, there are neighbours and bushwalkers combing the hills, forests, paddocks and beaches. I decided to take a look at a beach four kilometres away, and there in the far distance were two specks walking the beach, the dog and Dad. Somehow, they had met up with each other and headed for this beach, surrounded by steep sand dunes, and once

Dad was on the beach he could not climb out, so he and the dog had spent a couple of hours walking up and down.

5 November 1998: Some weeks later, still working on the house, not seeming such hard work. Dad is wandering around saying, 'Do you think you've taken on too much?' or 'Don't overdo it'. These comments all said the same thing to me, which was, 'You're going to fail'. So I said that was how I heard what he said, and he got shitty and moved away. I said that encouragement and positive statements would be more supportive, give me greater incentive to keep going.

Having spent most of my life listening to statements from my father about not overdoing it, like 'Don't do more than you are capable of' or 'Don't take on too much', this afternoon was probably the first time I had made a statement to Dad that said how I felt when he talked the way he did.

10 December 1998: I have had a very badly infected elbow, my forearm is blown up like a balloon. For the last four weeks, I have been on double doses of antibiotics and painkillers. Anyway, it's a lot better now; stopped me doing a lot. Dad came to me with what he called his 'dilemma'. Unable to remember where he was, what he was doing here. I asked him if he knew where he was and he said 'Tassie'. I asked what the date was. He said he could cheat and look it up, which he did, and came up with the fourth of December. I asked how old he thought he was. He thought for a while and said he was born in 1914 and if I gave him the date he could work it out. I insisted he have a guess and he came up with 87. I thought that pretty good. He was concerned with his memory loss. I said it was to do with memory and not his ability to think, which seemed okay. He wondered if he could teach podiatry. We worked out that he had stopped teaching nearly twenty years ago and was probably expecting too much to remember a lesson plan.

I talked about him having Alzheimer's and how at the moment there was no known treatment. I said, 'You're very fit, calm, and most of the time you are lucid'. We talked about what he would like to do. He thought he could start writing poetry again, but he was afraid to fail. I said if he left it much longer, he may lose the ability to put things on paper. We both have the same issue to deal with, fear of failing, so we both do nothing. 'Maybe,' I said, 'we could tell all of those people, who, when we were younger, kept saying we were hopeless, would never succeed and we could never do anything right, to go fuck themselves, and that they were wrong – we are succeeding.'

Dad understands at the time we talk, which is usually 3 a.m., but he mostly forgets. So we have these close intimate times that go unremembered by Dad, but I would still rather that, than not to have had these times at all.

20 December 1998: My elbow is much better, I was really worried that I may have caught a bug that was immune to the antibiotic. Wet start to the day. I have spent much of the night listening to Dad moving around, every two hours. He forgets to use his urine bottle and ends up pissing in the annex of the caravan. You have no idea what this smells like. I spent most of the day making up the inside of Christmas cards with dried flowers, which I did in the microwave.

Dad spends the whole day wandering around. He is looking for the fire. He has a wheelbarrow full of kindling and paper which he pushes in and out of the downstairs part of the house.

While he is eating lunch, I take the wheelbarrow upstairs where the fire is, and light the fire. I invite Dad to come up and watch TV or see a movie. He complains that the picture is bad. Gets up to go and get his glasses and that is the last I see of him until tea time. Dad thinks it is morning. Has he a doctor's appointment? Has he to go to the hospital? His wife is going to take him in. Dad repeats the question about ten times. My patience is stretched thin by this time and I have to watch my temper.

I have done nothing to the house for about four weeks. The garden is very dry. Next week is Christmas week.

13 January 1999: Christmas week went well. We spent Christmas Day with Ann and Terry Taylor and about eight others – Primo, Lisa, Keven, Karon, David, Lynne, Adam. Good food, played cricket and bowls. Interesting to play lawn bowls in a sheep paddock. New Year's Eve, down at the Tavern. The band 'Crunch' was playing – good music, good company, more good food. Fireworks and dancing. Dad wanted to go home after midnight; I could have gone on a bit longer.

New Year's Day, went in Terry's boat out to Big Dog Island, out from Lady Barron. Did a bit of snorkelling, good day, long day. One of Dad's often-quoted poems (not one of his):

There's a schooner in the bay with her topsails shot
With fire,
And my heart has gone aboard her for the Island
Of desire.

16 January 1999: Hot day, beautiful. Dad gets up, tries to go to the toilet. No go, constipated to the max. He stood on the veranda and said he did not know where he was standing. I have been talking to him about his trouble with remembering and having Alzheimer's. I have this idea that neither of us are letting go, holding on to sadness and pain, ending up distorting reality. By not acknowledging our issues, we block our repairing process. I keep wanting to talk with Robert or Steve, and I don't ring them, don't want to appear wanting. I miss my friends.

25 January 1999: I miss my mother, she and I were good friends. The thing is that every time he wakes, the change is still happening, a little bit more of what makes up my dad has gone. The long goodbye, and keeping a promise not to let Dad be put in a home. Contradiction in terms, 'home'. Anger and sadness have predominated my time looking after Dad.

26 January 1999: Fathers looking after their sons, somewhere, it changes to sons looking after their dads. Are we friends, companions, husband and wife, lovers? What happens to my life? I know of and have heard about many instances of daughters looking after fathers, mothers. Anyone who asks what I do and I say I'm a carer for my father, and they say, 'Ah! You're retired then'. Wouldn't the feminists love that twist.

I do the physical side of looking after my father reasonably well – making sure he has clean clothes, good food, warmth, shaved, finger- and toenails cut, medication, showers, laxatives. This is all left-brain stuff, male, easy, routine, in control. But to bring life into the relationship, giving dignity, respecting space, privacy, values, decisions, right of choice, taking time (really important) to move at his pace. Touching – my dad is no respecter of personal space. He touches because he wants to touch and won't respect or understand when someone (usually a woman) rears back from his approach. Yet he craves for this intimacy himself, melts into it. Age seems to create a wall, a barrier to touching, intimacy, hugging, holding a hand. Dad gets so tense across the shoulders he cuts off the circulation to his hands. Is this the reason why grandparents get close to grandchildren, because they have the time and it's okay to get close?

I had a week to myself. Dad stayed with a couple on the east coast, 'respite care' it's called. Anyway, I used the time to get the plumbing finished. Now we have hot water, our own shower, after fourteen months of bucket showers on the veranda, which can be great on warm days - even Dad would have one - but not when the wind blows.

The more I write this journal, diary, whatever, the clearer a lot of issues become. That is what is supposed to happen and I feel good that it is.

Because when I feel okay, I see the reflection in my dad: more smiles, sighs of contentment, freer attitude of tolerance, connection grows, and there is a possible prospect of a rich harvest.

He is not the dad I remember or think I had, but we are the same

> He is not the dad I remember ... but we are the same blood and ... this seems important, a good reason to be together.

blood and somehow, in all the decay of my dad's mind, this seems important, a good reason to be together.

Out of his loss of memory and logic, he is living every day for the first time. He sees the same sun, mountains and sea every day for the first time. In his eyes, a child's wonderment. I'm envious of that. My mother once talked of being 'bird happy' and I knew what she meant, I could remember what that felt like. I want that still.

27 January 1999, a.m.: I've been thinking about how I would pay out on my dad, take advantage of his state of mind, to work off some of my own bloody-mindedness or whatever else was going on in my head. Because I would not face some of my own issues, I'd use my dad as a way of distracting myself. So if I was feeling low, which manifests itself in me as surly and picky, I would be angry and surly at my father. My father, who has a good bullshit detector, would respond in kind, and he could be equally, if not more so, as stubborn and vitriolic as I was.

I provoked these scenes quite often, then, for some reason which I think was sparked off by someone's remark about giving dignity to those less fortunate, I took a long hard look at what I was doing and I took responsibly for what I was doing. I decided to stop; you have no idea how hard it is to stop doing the behaviour. The relationship between us is much better. I listen to what Dad is saying and I take time to respond to him, rather than reacting to him and venting something in me.

It is not just the way my dad has changed and what he has become that I have accepted. It is what I am, how I behave and deal with relationships that I now realise has blocked any movement in my own life. There were long moments, in the last two years, when I thought I had developed a personal torture system to wreck my life. Not so, of course, just my refusal to look at what I was doing, how I was behaving. Now I have accepted what I need to do, I do feel better and what occurs between Dad and me is very much better.

1 February 1999: Birthday, 54 years old. Just another day, same routines.

3 February 1999: Woke up hot, depressed. I don't think very well, there seems such a lot to do. I have a constant backache, so when I work, I'm always in pain. I know what I need to do – lose weight, exercise. Here I go, into self-loathing, fear of failing – what a combination to waste time. Just do it! Watching a fairy wren, a young one, female, bouncing around, tail is so upright, so much up that it nearly taps her on the back of her head when she moves. Two black-backed gulls, mollyhawks, glide across the sky just above the trees, slowly sliding on the wind, taking in all below.

I talk with Dad about him doing some writing and he takes off on a flight of words that run into each other, tumble into the air and have no meaning for me. I feel sad; it's possibly too late for Dad to leave a legacy of his poetry and writing.

It's a beautiful day, breezy, warm air wafting, sometimes quietly, sometimes busy and noisy, moving wind chimes to symphonic discord. There are two layers of clouds. One high, paint-brushed onto a blue canvas. The other lower, rounded, woolly. Both move so slowly to be stopped, suspended. What is happening here? Seems to be a need to stimulate, be stimulated. There are a lot of things to do. No motivation, feelings of depression, lassitude, boredom, guilt, pressure to have to finish the house, look after Dad, cook tea, do the laundry. Feeling angry at having to, *got to*, must, should. Bugger me. Rang some of my friends tonight. I got three things: many fears are born of fatigue and loneliness; just do it; ring a friend a day.

If I was to be asked what I would tell men who are thinking of looking after their dads, I'd say: just loving each other is not enough, you need to be friends, like each other.

4 February 1999: Bike ride - morning, lots of sweat and hard work. But it's good. I will keep going

Postscript

23 July 2000: Fifteen months later, my father is in a home for the aged, getting better care and attention than I was able to provide. Dad went into the home in April 2000.

Reviewing what I have written, over twelve months later, I see I have moved on - or moved through - to a much calmer place. The anger I felt towards Dad has gone, replaced by an acceptance, and peace. The decision was hard for me. I thought I was weak, that I was letting my dad down. I felt guilty. But I was putting in 24 hours a day, and it was no life for me. Interestingly, though, Dad is now happier, more contented, and certainly better cared-for. He fitted into the place as if he had been there all his life. People call in to see him, talk to him, take him for walks, take him for a drive, take him out for a cup of tea.

The sense of community over this island is like nothing I have ever experienced. I do not mean I am in a state of euphoria - I am well aware of the realities of a small community. I mean, I am overwhelmed sometimes when this community moves as one in an act of care and concern for either an individual or the whole community. I could not have planned a better place for my father if I had tried to dream one up.

As for me, I'm flat out like a lizard drinking. The week Dad went into the centre, I applied for two part-time jobs and got them, and a short time later, picked up a third. So now I am a water-watcher, a coordinator for adventure weekends for young people, and a part-time tutor at the district high school. Do I get to see my father? Not as often as I want to, so I am going to give up one of my jobs, otherwise I will end up right back where I began. I want to enjoy what time is left with my dad, and I also want to have a life – not easy, but entirely possible.

Die with dignity

Michael Leunig

Mary Pipher, in her important and perceptive book *Another Country*, details how the care of the elderly today reflects the terrible loss of community in the suburban world, and how the commercialisation of medicine is fraught with the potential for mistakes, callousness and indignity for us as we grow old.

Leunig, of course, manages to say this with just a few squiggly lines.

Remembering Mowaljarlai

John Allan

One of the blessings of my life was to spend some time with Aboriginal elder David Mowaljarlai. When David died several years ago, he took with him knowledge more valuable than entire libraries of books. His life had spanned the traditional times, the coming of the missionaries, the terrible evictions from the land to make way for cattle, and the long struggle to keep the young people alive and regain the sacred places – a struggle that is still going on today.

David Mowaljarlai taught that the job of a man is to protect and care for all the life around him. That teaching has since defined my life, and given it cohesion, purpose and a joyful sense of belonging. It is still not possible for me to read his words without beginning to cry. My tears are in appreciation of his life, and from grief at the ongoing pain of his people.

Mowaljarlai ... I will call him the Old Man now that he has passed, but you will know who I mean. In 1994, Rein van der Ruit and I were planning a men's gathering. Rein organised for him to be at Kevin Shaw's house in Derby where we rang him. Rein had helped the Old Man many years before when they were setting up the Kamali Land Council, and, before that, getting the first excision of land in WA for a community from a pastoral lease.

We told him about the work we were doing with men and boys – the bush gatherings we organised – and asked if he would come over to northern NSW from the Kimberley. His immediate reply was: 'You helped me with my people, now I will come and help you with your people'. We called the gathering 'Everyone Standing Up Alive' from the Wandjina Law of Yorro Yorro, as a mark of respect. (We still use the name, as he said to.)

Over 70 men came and an extraordinary sharing happened. He was a highly initiated man – a Law Man – and spontaneously did the teaching and blessing work of an elder. A local traditional owner of the land welcomed us to the site. The Old Man thanked him and talked about how beautiful the land in the Northern Rivers is. Then he said, 'Everything here in this creation is standing up alive and beautiful, and because *all of you* are part of it, *you* are beautiful, too. *All you have to do is remember that.*' It was said so simply, but it carried an enormous power of blessing that shook many of the men.

From his frame of reference, we had set up a Law Gathering, different from what he had grown up with, but the same in spirit, and he acted accordingly. It was his genius to go for the heart of things and, like a true artist and teacher, improvise on his enormous wealth of traditional wisdom to meet the moment, always remaining true to the essence.

The big turning point, from just talking about culture and law to enactment of it, came on the first day. The Old Man told the story of Wodoi and Djingun and how they had stolen some sacred objects from even more ancient inhabitants of the land. Like all culture heroes and tricksters, they didn't steal for personal profit. After making amends with the true owners, they used the objects as power symbols to start a new Law – the Wunnan sharing system. They did all this because their people were dying from not knowing how to live on the land.

They started the Wunnan, the sharing system, with the first two branches of a network of 'lines', or pathways that some call 'songlines'. Eventually, this sharing system embraced all of Australia. The Old Man told the story to the point where Emu comes from the East and steals sacramental food that the ancestral beings are sharing, one after another, to show their commitment to the new Law. Emu, like all materialists, is greedy and won't wait, stealing all the sacramental food for personal gain.

In the traditional way, the Old Man gave no interpretation. You had to work it out for yourself that ending the story at this point emphasised the conflict of values that happens in the heart from moment to moment – and which happened with white contact, an historical tragedy.

He taught that the lines of the Wunnan sharing system are a network over the entire continent.

'The lines of the sharing system are still there. Though different people live on them. We have to build a new Wunnan so there can be right relationships between all people in the country ... If you live in this land and take care of it, then you belong here. We want to share the knowledge of how to look after the land. The songs from the totems that go with the land are wisdom that is very important for people to pick up and understand. We're not saying you must come as a full Aboriginal – no, we're not saying that, but to share knowledge. We're all human beings, we can share the knowledge.'

Using playback theatre, I directed the men to enact moments from their lives that were sparked by this; or to identify with the beings in the Wodoi and Djinjun story and enact moments in the story from a first-person position. The Old Man was watching intently, and then he was up and directing us in a full re-enactment of the Wunnan story. He became full of life, directing 70 men in the enactment, running around the paddock like a young man. He had told these stories and shared his wealth of knowledge in universities and many other places over the years, but this was different.

When he saw how we enacted the story, he seemed to come to a decision. *Here is a mob of white men who will play, who will dance and do it*. So he pulled out all the stops and got us enacting the law stories. As one man said later, 'I thought I would come along and learn something about Aboriginal culture. I never thought I would be invited *in*!'

This is the open secret of traditional Aboriginal culture. The enactment of sacred stories through dance, drama and song *is* the primary spiritual practice; you become the ancestral beings through enactment. And it is communal. Yes, some things are very secret and separate from the general community, but much is shared by men, women and children. By singing the songs and doing the dances, it is possible to enter into ecstatic communion with the ancestors, and, since ancestral beings are also all species, you are in communion with all creation.

'This law is hard for white people to understand – it's all linked up. When you consider one part, you've got to have all the rest of it in your heart, not separate it out.'

He brought us a carved pearl shell, a *Jagali* – a symbol of the Wunnan sharing system and a symbol of what he wanted to share. The particular pattern on this shell is the one that is sent along the lines of the Wunnan when there is a problem. Everyone has to come together and sort it out. Under the law of this symbol, everyone is obliged to speak straight to the point to work problems out without delay.

'We used it in the formal times [when] we have to speak of strong feeling and thoughts. Men spoke of things in their lives and community that brought tears, and of things that brought smiles.'

Then the Old Man held the *Jagali* and spoke. He said it was the first time he had seen white men cry, and then spoke of the things that weighed heavily with him. His people being moved away from their land during World War II and into the 1950s. All the losses that followed, the Law Men and Women slowly passing – and with them the Law.

'Once we old fellas die, with our history and stories, and we are buried with it, well, it will be burning, burning for the rest of time and no-one will ever know of it.'

The greatest sadness came when he told of the deaths of so many young people caught in hopelessness and dying from the

grog and drugs and suicide. There were tears in his eyes when he spoke of this – asking why would the government take the people from the land when all this happened. Then, 'Seeing it happen, why do they make us fight so hard to get it back?' He said it was the first time he had ever showed tears to white men.

He asked me to read two poems from his book *Yorro Yorro: Everything standing up alive*. The first poem was a song of how it was, how it is, and how it can be for his people, the Worora, Ngarinyin and Wunambal of the Kimberley.

I am Worora
I am Ngarinyin
I am Wunambal
Once I walked in my country
But lost my place
Then I lost my dignity-spirit.

Once when I walked my country
I was lizard and kangaroo
I was turkey and emu
And the Wandjina walked with me.

Now I have lost my place
I am grog and despair
I am sickness and early death
And Wandjina can't walk in jails.

How did I leave my country
What brought me out of my land
Can I remember
Did I ever know?

I must remember, I must know
Might be an illusion
That holds me from my country.

For I am Worora
I am lizard and kangaroo
I am turkey and emu
And I am spirit-rock
And I am Wandjina.

The second poem was a short call from the heart about his and other elders' pain at the loss of so much.

Once I was past and future
now I am only the present
today, the moment
and that is hard to bear
with no past, no future.

He was constantly trying to find ways to get the young people away from the towns and into the bush where he and other senior elders could teach them. This task was made the more difficult by the death, or complete loss to alcohol, of so many of the in-between generation – the younger elders.

'Everything is upside-down. I am doing jobs for young men when they should be doing jobs for old people. We really old people are still giving when we should be receiving. We are standing over a young man's grave when they should be standing over ours.'

Faced with such tragedy, including the loss of some of his own children, many people who met him wondered how he had the strength to carry on with such patience and spiritual presence. He said it was because of the foundation he received as a child.

I asked him about his main memory and feeling from childhood, and he talked about joy.

'I was serving at that time, getting firewood and cooking kangaroo for old people, for anybody. When we were in a hunting area and a man brought a kangaroo, I would jump up and collect wood, and dig a hole. That was my job. I felt proud, and the old people, they feel really proud because they wouldn't have to tell me to do this and that, because I had learnt. The community was my family, it was my culture, my responsibility to learn.

'I was learning to grow up with a good heart. I wanted the old people to be proud of me and they blessed me and praised me. I was really happy – I was filled up. It was really a time of great joy; I couldn't have been happier.

'It gave me a good start in life so I could control myself. I really appreciate that. And now, today, I can still hear those old people talking to me. I hear their voices. Really! From mother, uncle or granny [a *granny* is a person who teaches you law – male or female], all of them. I can still hear them talking to me, *wherever* I go. That's very precious to me.

'That's how we learnt, and even in my old age, they are still talking to me. It's stayed with me like glue; it's glued in my body, in my mind. This is how I am today. This great start in life is how I began. When the drinking started in the Seventies with the citizenship rights, people with my training were able to resist it better than the younger ones, who didn't have our training and life experience. So when that alcohol business came, *my life was able to hold me solid as a rock* [against it].

'Among the pressure and the life changes, I can hear my ancestors keep talking to me. The younger ones [growing up at a time when the traditions based on the deep Aboriginal connection with the land were disintegrating, due to the land being taken away] don't have the sound of the ancestors in their mind talking to them. They have nothing and they are lost. They can't hold up against anything. This is very important. That's what makes me sad. They don't want to listen to me. I have to take them away, out bush, away from alcohol, otherwise they've got wet brains seven days a week. When they are dried out, you got to fill them up with something. Got to plant seeds of wisdom in dry brains, no alcohol. You can't do it with alcohol around, learning just slips away. They get hooked on it, addicted – wrecked livers and kidneys. They die from it. Once they're on it, they are really on it – can't get off. They are always broke. They can't stand up against it all – can't decide anything, but just go along with it all.'

The Old Man taught us that the path of initiation is a lifelong thing. It is not about accumulating power or status, it's about taking on deeper and deeper levels of responsibility and commitment to service. The first initiation doesn't make you a man; it puts you on the inside of the Wunnan sharing system so you can start taking on responsibilities.

At a commitment ceremony – that we always have as a part of Standing Up Alive gatherings – he said, 'When I was a young man, I spilt my blood on the earth as a covenant to serve my community, my people. I have faithfully done this all my life. Now, in the time before I go on my last journey, I reaffirm it and extend it to include all people, everywhere.'

Mowaljarlai was a great and learned man who worked with several generations of anthropologists. He spoke at least eight different indigenous languages as well as English, and learnt the lore of many tribal groups. He acted as a Law Man to many communities. In the face of enormous difficulties, he made journeys to his country, even though he had been moved hundreds of miles from it. Because of his commitment to service, he worked tirelessly on behalf of his people. In spite of all the injustice he had to contend with, he stayed true to the Wandjina way of open-heartedness, and resisted the temptation to lapse into bitterness or hopeless despair. He wanted to share deep traditional wisdom so that real understanding could grow and the land would be cared for in the proper ways. He truthfully called the land 'his people's sacred book'. He used to say, 'When I'm on a high mountain, looking out over the country, my unggur [life force] flows out from inside my body, and I fall open with happiness.'

Now he is gone, I still hear him talking in my heart. His strong and gentle presence is part of this land reminding me to keep my heart open, to be of service and to stay creative and committed.

Rescue in East Timor

Major John Petrie with Barbie Dutter

With the cold war over, a rash of small and ugly wars has broken out around the world, reminding us of the urgent need for development aid to promote stability and peace. The need for intervention is great, even if this means men with guns to stop the killing. In East Timor, this lesson was learnt, but not quickly enough to prevent many thousands of innocent deaths. In the story that follows, two UN liaison officers smuggle 30 people to safety at great risk to themselves. It's told without ornamentation, so their heroism stands out all the more starkly. I sometimes think that the world gets through each day because of one reason alone – that certain men and women do more than is actually asked of them.

The first time I really saw the people's fear was on the afternoon of September 3, when it was announced that the election results would be given a day early. They were pleading with us to get them out because they fully believed that they were going to be killed by the militia and the Indonesian Army the following day.

We wanted to get some people to Uaimori, a mountain area protected by the pro-independence fighters – and others, particularly women and children, to the church. This was personal, not professional. My Brazilian UN colleague and I had genuine affection for our host family. We felt we owed it to them to ensure that they were safe.

The first run was in daylight, at about 4 p.m. We put four men in the back of the Land Rover, lying head-to-toe. We covered them with a green tarpaulin, then put boxes of bottled water on top. Three young children and their mother were wedged into the wells between the front and rear seats. We put our military rucksacks on the back seat so they could not be seen.

To get to the village in Uaimori [Cairui], we had to go through a militia roadblock, a checkpoint manned by the Indonesian army and past two army observation posts. We were stopped almost immediately by the heavily armed militia and we asked them to open the checkpoint for us. They prevaricated for about 30 seconds. It seemed like forever. One of them walked down the side of the car. I thought, *This is it.* We put the central locking on so that they couldn't open the back door.

There were twelve of them, seven on one side, five on the other. I was aware of every movement. It was almost as though it was happening in slow motion. I would have expected to be absolutely petrified in a situation like that, but for some reason I was absolutely lucid. The only weapon we had in the car was my NATO jungle knife. I pulled it out ready. If one of the militia had reached into the car with a weapon, I was prepared to chop off his arm and drive away.

My Brazilian colleague was brilliant. He spoke to a couple of the militia in Portuguese to make it appear that everything was normal. In the end, they waved us through. We knew that the army checkpoint wasn't very far away. But they were easier to deal with because they recognised us immediately as UN military liaison officers. When we had slowed down a bit and they saw who we were, they called us straight through.

After the few army observation posts, there was then a twenty-minute drive down a rough track alongside the river to the village of Cairui. We crossed the riverbed to the point where our passengers were going to be met by the independence fighters and escorted up to Uaimori. When we got back to Manatuto, what we were doing had spread by word of mouth. There was a group of locals waiting for us. We did two runs to the Catholic church in the town, because that was where the women and children had felt they would be protected by the priest. Each time, we had four women in the boot and four children between the back and front seats.

The first journey to the church was no problem: the militias waved us straight through. They probably assumed we were going to the UN building because we were headed in that direction. We drove round behind the church. The people got out and went inside. Then we went straight back and picked up the next lot. But this time when we got to the militia checkpoint, they stopped us. This was a worry because it was dusk, but it wasn't dark enough for there to be complete cover in the back of our vehicle. I could feel one of the children, a girl of about five or six, shaking and whimpering behind me. I thought she was going to cry. I had a tape in the deck, which I turned up, and had this utterly bizarre experience of Vivaldi's *Four Seasons* being played while we were stopped at a militia checkpoint.

The head of the militia at that point was a big, fat man who terrorised the population. He had just arrived at the checkpoint and we got held there. They weren't going to let us through. My colleagues called them round to the other side of the vehicle, which allowed me to get my knife out in case anything happened. Fortunately, one of the militia leaders arrived at that point and just called us through. We went to the church, dropped the people off and went back home.

We really did not want to have to do another run at that point. If we had been caught at another checkpoint, they would have killed us, there is no question about that. But when we got back there were about six people from the little corner where we lived waiting for us. They pleaded with us to do a final run to Cairui. They didn't

> If we had been caught at another checkpoint, they would have killed us, there is no question about that.

want to go to the church because the men believed they would
be killed there.

We waited for a while, until it was dark. We got our kit, put
it in the car and put these people in for the final run. There
were four men in the back and one each between the front and
back seats.

By this time, the army had started patrolling around the area,
although we didn't know it at the time. At the first checkpoint,
there were about eighteen militia. That was the single worst
moment of all, because we were stopped behind another vehicle,
which meant we were going to be kept there for a while.

As we waited, the militia came up and gathered around. They
started leaning against the sides of the vehicle. In order to stop
them, I got out of the driver's seat and walked away. I pretended
to be interested in their guns.

You could sense that the people hidden in our car were
starting to panic. We were held there for nearly four minutes.
The previous vehicle was a little local minibus. The militia had
opened the back and checked inside looking for specific
people. If they had done that to us, we would have been
finished. As soon as the other vehicle pulled off, we got in,
revved up, and moved up to the militia point. We didn't stop,
because we weren't going to give them the chance of holding
us at the barrier.

So we drove on out there. But nobody drives to Cairui at
night unless they are independence fighters. A platoon of army
soldiers based down there saw the lights from our vehicle. They
came out onto the side of the road. As we drove past, we leaned
out and greeted them and they just waved us past. We drove

back and there was a deathly hush in Manatuto. Everybody had gone to ground. We were the only vehicle moving except for the militia's motorcycles. That was really the beginning of the end of the Manatuto business. The following morning we had to go to the office for the election results at 9 a.m. By 9.45, the first attack on the UN building had started. There were three attacks. We were evacuated to Baucau the following day at 11 o'clock.

I was unable to talk about those few days at first because I had this huge guilty dread that the people we helped were all going to be dead. There was a psychological block, and I could not acknowledge that what I had done had been worth the risk until I knew that they were still alive. When I went up to Uaimori on a UN flight last week, there were shouts of 'Mr John, Mr John', and I saw the mother, grandmother and children of the family we had stayed with, who had been taken on our first run to Cairui. I had a huge lump in my throat. I walked across to where the crowds were, and when I got closer they saw me and came running up. The mother put her arms around me and sobbed into my chest for five minutes.

Then the kids came up and said, 'Hello, Mr John'. They had wonderful smiley faces and big shiny eyes, just as if nothing had happened. It was unbelievable. They had gone through hell, yet they wanted lots of cuddles and to be picked up. It was just like being back at their house, reading them stories that they couldn't understand. That was the first time I was certain that the risk had been worthwhile. If they had all been dead, if there had been a massacre in the church as we had been told there had been, I would never have accepted that I had made the right decision. And most importantly, I would have taken that risk in vain, without considering that my two sons, Harry and Guy, might have been left without their father.

Notes

Introduction

The poems by Val Maslen (who writes under the name Val French) appear in *A Treasury of Insights and Memories*. Copies of this highly recommended book can be purchased from the author. Write to Val Maslen, 37 Downing Street, Hove, South Australia 5048, or send an e-mail to: robmas@dove.net.au

A boys' world, tears and all

Simon Carr is the author of *The Boys are Back in Town*, to be published by Hutchinson (London).

A small child's needs

Mankind News is a bi-monthly newsletter published by a small men's group, Mankind Albury. Charles Fransen or Mankind Albury may be contacted at P O Box 3364, Albury, NSW 2460 or at mankindalbury@hotmail.com

It's a snip

Ian Hargreaves is a broadcaster and journalist, and a former editor of *The Independent* and *New Statesman*. He is also Professor of Journalism at Cardiff University in Wales.

No, brother

Leo Schofield is a Sydney writer, Director of the Sydney Festival and Artistic Director of the Sydney 2000 Olympic Arts Festival.

Broken Rites is a self-help and support group for people sexually abused by clergy and religious orders. Their address is P O Box 163, Rosanna, Victoria. Phone (03) 9457 4999.

The Catholic Church in Australia also has a support and information service for people sexually abused by priests or brothers. This service was set up as part of its reconciliation efforts for victims. Towards Healing can be contacted on (03) 9580 4515.

Things we wouldn't know without TV

This piece of wry humour comes from *Small Screen,* the newsletter of Young Media Australia, the film and television watchdog that makes a brave attempt to stem the tide of trash directed at children. Young Media Australia can be visited at www.youngmedia.orga.au. The piece originally appeared in 'Clipboard', the Canadian media education newsletter.

John J Pungente, SJ, is President of the Canadian Association of Media Education Organisations, a Jesuit and a TV show host in Canada.

My goofy brother

The Big Sister/Big Brother program is a friendship and mentoring program for disadvantaged children operated by the YWCA. They urgently need more volunteers. The YWCA may be contacted on 1800 222 776; their web site is www.bigsisterbigbrotherprogram.com.au

The sporting life

This article first appeared in the *Mail on Sunday's Night and Day* magazine between 6 October 1996 and 17 May 1998.

Love in the time of economic rationalism

Elliot Perlman was born in 1964. He won *The Age* Short Story Competition for 'The Reasons I Won't be Coming' in 1994. His novel *Three Dollars* won *The Age* Book of the Year Award, the Betty Trask Award (UK) and was the joint winner of the FAW Book of the Year Award. He lives in Melbourne where he works as a barrister.

Women teaching boys

This story is extracted from a monograph, published as *Women Teaching Boys: The Confessions of Nancy Lerner.* Nancy Lerner taught

English at University School, Hunting Valley, Ohio, from 1989 through 1994 and was a visiting faculty fellow for 1994-95. She was educated at Case Western Reserve University, where she received her BA, MA and PhD. For the material in her *Confessions*, she is indebted to her colleagues at University School, Carol Pribble, Margaret Mason and Jannie Brown; to Shirley Anderson, former teacher at University School, now teaching in Washington State; and especially to Ann Behrman, former head of the English Department at University School, now with Stanford University.

page 114 **'These *Confessions* ...'** *The Confessions of Nancy Lerner.*

page 116 **'Walt the Wild Man'** Throughout this essay, pseudonyms replace students' names.

page 117 **'*[base] their preferences ... they will cause trouble*'** Richard A. Hawley, 'Three Hopes for a Boys' School', remarks on the occasion of Roxbury Latin's 350th Anniversary, Boston, 7 April 1995.

page 118 **'the leading cause of violence is maleness'** Robert Wright, 'The Biology of Violence', *The New Yorker*, 13 March 1995, 68-77. (The quotation is from a 1994 paper by Martin Daly and Margo Wilson cited by Wright.)

page 118 **'such negative images of masculinity'** Richard A. Hawley, *Boys Will Be Men: Masculinity in Troubled Times*, Middlebury, VT, 1993, p. 3.

page 118 **'or Richard Hawley's liberated feminist ...'** Hawley, *Boys will be Men*, p. 4.

page 124 **'Studies have shown ... "little confidence in their own ability to speak"'** Mary Field Belenky, Blythe McVicker Clinchy, Nancy Rule Goldberger & Jill Mattuck Tarule, *Women's Ways of Knowing: The Development of Self, Voice, and Mind*, New York, 1986, p. 37.

page 124 **'for females who "fear failing in front of males"'** 'Studies Link Subtle Sex Bias in Schools with Women's Behaviour in the Workplace', *The Wall Street Journal*, 16 September 1988.

page 126 **'Girls probably ... because they cared more about my feelings'** Carol Gilligan & Edith Phelps, *Seeking Connections: New*

Insights and Questions for Teachers, Harvard Graduate School of
Education, August, 1988: 'Females were more likely to suppress their
true feelings to avoid hurting others …', p. 7.

page 126 **'girls learn they must "balance drive with deference"
to succeed.'** David Halberstam, 'Popular, Pretty, Polite, Not Too
Smart', rev. of *Schoolgirls: Women, Self-Esteem and the Confidence
Gap* by Peggy Orenstein, *The New York Times Book Review*, 11
September 1994, p. 16.

page 127 **'… the Gilligan and Phelps' 1988 report on boys …'**
Gilligan & Phelps, p.7.

No sweet dreams in the small hours

The book *Another Country* by Mary Pipher, published by Random
House, is an excellent campaign manual for the elderly, and a practical
guide for their families.

The last time I hit a woman

In relation to domestic violence, I recommend Christine Hoff Sommer's
book, *Who Stole Feminism?* (Simon & Schuster, New York, 1995).

Die with dignity

Mary Pipher's book, *Another Country: Navigating the emotional
terrain of our elders*, is published by Doubleday (Sydney, 1999).

Remembering Mowaljarlai

John Allan kindly wrote this tribute specifically for this book in July
2000. We appreciate his help in providing it. In the Aboriginal way,
after a certain time when a person has died, their name is no longer
spoken or written down. Because of Mowaljarlai's high profile, his
people realise that his name needs to be referred to, so, in his case, they
waived the traditional time of silence. We apologise if feelings of grief
arise from his memory being evoked, and hope that the importance of
his teaching and purpose make publication the right thing to have done.

Acknowledgements

The editor and the publisher gratefully acknowledge permission to reproduce copyright works in this book.

Scott Adams: from *The Dilbert Future, Thriving on Business Stupidity in the 21st Century*, New York. Copyright © 1997 by United Media, Inc. Reprinted by permission of HarperCollins Publishers, Inc.

John Allan: 'Remembering Mowaljarlai'. Text copyright © John Allan 2000. Used with permission. Poems from *Yorro Yorro: Everything standing up alive* by David Mowaljarlai and Jutta Malnic, published by Magabala Books Aboriginal Corporation, Broome, Western Australia, 1993.

J J Bell: 'The Good Fairy' (short story) originally published in *Kiddies*, Mills and Boon. Published in *Growing up in Scotland*, Selection and Introduction © 1998 Robbie & Nora Kydd, Edinburgh. Every reasonable effort has been made to contact the copyright holder.

Bill Brandt: 'Home from the Mine', image 'The Coal Miner's Bath', Chester-le-Street, Durham, 1937. Copyright © Bill Brandt. Reproduced by permission of Bill Brandt Archive.

Bill Bryson: from *I'm a Stranger Here Myself* by Bill Bryson, copyright © 1999 by Bill Bryson. Used by permission of Broadway Books, a division of Random House, Inc., New York. Extracted from *Notes from a Big Country* by Bill Bryson, a Black Swan Book published by Transworld Publishers Ltd, London. All rights reserved.

Peter Carey: reprinted by permission of International Creative Management, Inc. Copyright © 2000 Peter Carey. This article was first published in *The New Yorker* magazine, New York, and also appeared in *The Australian Magazine* on 14 October 1995.

Simon Carr: this article first appeared in *The Daily Telegraph* newspaper, London, UK, 3 December 1998. Copyright © Simon Carr. Reprinted with kind permission of Simon Carr.

Bob Ellis: from *The Age* newspaper, Melbourne, 20 February 1998. Copyright © Bobon Entertainment Services. Reprinted with kind permission of Bobon Entertainment Services.

Charles Fransen: from *Mankind News*, p.3, October 1998, Albury, NSW. Copyright © Charles Fransen. Reprinted with kind permission of Charles Fransen.

Ian Hargreaves: from *The Daily Mail* newspaper, London, UK, of 25 September 1999. This article first appeared in the September 1999 edition of *Prospect Magazine* (UK). Copyright © Ian Hargreaves. Reprinted with kind permission of Ian Hargreaves.

Mohamed H Khadra: from the *Medical Journal of Australia*, Sydney, 6 July 1998, vol. 169. Copyright © Mohamed Khadra. Reprinted with kind permission of Mohamed Khadra.

Nancy Lerner: an abridged version of the mongraph entitled *Women Teaching Boys:The Confessions of Nancy Lerner* published in 1995. Copyright © 1995 The University School Press, Hunting Valley, Ohio. All rights reserved.

Michael Leunig: four cartoons from *You & Me*, Penguin Books Australia Ltd, Ringwood, Victoria. Copyright © Michael Leunig 1995. Reprinted by permission of Penguin Books Australia Ltd.

Val Maslen: 'Memories of a father', from *A Treasury of Insights and Memories*, Peacock Press, Adelaide, 1998. Copyright © Val Maslen. Reprinted with kind permission of Val Maslen.

Simon McCulloch: Copyright © Simon McCulloch.

Adam Mitchell: Copyright © Adam Mitchell.

Alden Nowlan: 'The Rites of Manhood', originally published in *I'm a Stranger Here Myself*. Copyright © 1974 Clarke, Irwin Co. Ltd. Reprinted by permission of Irwin Publishing Incorporated. Rights administered by Stoddart Publishing Co. Limited, Toronto, Ontario, Canada.

Elliot Perlman: from the *Good Weekend* magazine of *The Sydney Morning Herald*, Sydney, 29 August 1998. Copyright © Elliot Perlman. Reprinted with kind permission of Elliot Perlman.

The story behind the cover

In September 1965 I was on a photographic assignment for *National Geographic* in Central Australia. Prolonged drought had seared the land creating a dustbowl of shifting sand.

Flying in to the Central Mount Wedge station I was greeted by Bill Wardby and his son Bobby. Wardby epitomised the character and stoicism of outback folk. Bobby was learning about hard work and hardship as he grew to be like his dad. They were self-reliant in the remote vastness of the land.

David Moore

Recommendations from Steve Biddulph

If you liked the stories in this book, there are two offerings you might enjoy following up. Amazingly, they both have the same name, though there is no other connection.

CERTIFIED**M**ALE

Certified Male is a magazine about men's lives, their relationships with women, children and other men, politics and the law as it affects men, boys becoming men, and the men's movement. It is very much based on men's stories about their real-life experiences.

It has been going since 1995 and averages two to three issues per year. It is available by subscription only. For details see www.certifiedmale.org To subscribe for four issues, send $22 to Locked Bag 1, Springwood, NSW 2777. Phone (02) 4751 1127; fax (02) 4751 5518.

This hit stage show is now touring both Australia and overseas, and might be in a city near you very soon. Don't miss it! Written by Glynn Nicholas and Scott Rankin, and loosely based on *Manhood*, it is hilarious, wise, touching and liberating.

"… it works beautifully … classy … beautifully drawn (and hilarious) … it's probably fair to say that blokes don't often get dissected with this level of empathy and comic detail." *The Sydney Morning Herald*

"It is one of the brightest, funniest, and cleverest pieces in town ... riotously funny" *Australian Jewish News*

Information from Finch Publishing

Raising boys

In his international bestseller, author Steve Biddulph examines the crucial ways that boys differ from girls. He looks at boys' development from birth to manhood and discusses the parenting and guidance boys need to develop into well balanced and happy men.

Raising Boys: Why boys are different – and how to help them become happy and well-balanced men by Steve Biddulph. ISBN 0 646 31418 1

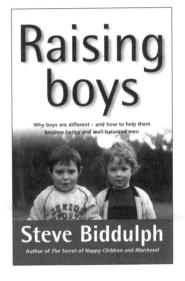

Manhood

This bestselling book has had a profound effect on the lives of thousands of men and women around the world. Steve Biddulph discusses issues such as love and sexuality, being a father, finding meaning in work, making real friends, forming new partnerships with women and honouring our own needs.

Manhood: An action plan for changing men's lives (2nd ed.) by Steve Biddulph ISBN 0 646 261 44 4

Other Finch titles

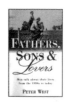

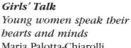

Side by Side
*How to think differently
about your relationship*
Jo Lamble and Sue Morris
ISBN 1876451092

Beginning Fatherhood
*A guide for expectant
fathers*
Warwick Pudney and Judy
Cottrell
ISBN 1876451017

The Body Snatchers
*How the media shapes
women*
Cyndi Tebbel
ISBN 1876451076

Boys in Schools
*Addressing the real issues
– behaviour, values and
relationships*
Rollo Browne and Richard
Fletcher
ISBN 0646239589

Bullybusting
*How to help children deal
with teasing and bullying*
Evelyn Field
ISBN 1876451041

Dealing with Anger
Self-help solutions for men
Frank Donovan
ISBN 187645105X

Fathers After Divorce
*Building a new life and
becoming a successful
separated parent*
Michael Green
ISBN 1876451009

Fathers, Sons and Lovers
*Men talk about their lives
from 1930s to today*
Dr Peter West
ISBN 0646288164

Girls' Talk
*Young women speak their
hearts and minds*
Maria Palotta-Chiarolli
ISBN 1876451025

Motherhood
Making it work for you
Jo Lamble and Sue Morris
ISBN 1876451033

On Their Own
*Boys growing up
underfathered*
Rex McCann
ISBN 1876451092

Parentcraft
*Essential skills for
raising children from
infancy to adulthood*
Ken and Elizabeth Mellor
ISBN 1876451068

Finch titles are available in bookshops or at www.finch.com.au